An Evidence-based Approach to Authentic Leadership Development

This book presents the first evidence-based approach to Authentic Leadership Development. It is based on a group coaching format that brings together small groups of leaders to discuss personally significant leadership issues generally not explored in usual leadership development, such as the influence of their personal histories, the impact of their psychological make-up and the ambitions for their future leadership.

The book starts with an overview of the idea of authenticity and its philosophical roots and explains how this informs the past/present/future group coaching approach to Authentic Leadership Development. It presents statistical and conceptual evidence of the programme's efficacy and explores how the social processes at work within the group positively impact and develop the leader's self-concept and the benefits this brings. Importantly, it also details exactly how the leader changes and grows as a result of the group coaching and the positive ways in which this benefits their leadership role and the organisations they work in. Finally, it questions the notion of ethics and morals in Authentic Leadership and critically reappraises the idea of leadership development evaluation. Authentic Leadership Development group coaching has been shown to develop leaders that are conscious, competent, confident and congruent and as the qualitative analysis presented in the book illustrates, these four overarching categories are made up of seven further key leadership attributes that are developed, which include an enhanced Strategic Orientation, increased Confidence and Clarity and greater Management Mindfulness, among others. The book also features personal vignettes throughout, which illustrate how individual leaders have effectively applied these newly developed attributes in their leadership roles.

An Evidence-based Approach to Authentic Leadership Development represents essential reading for leaders who want to engage in a 'proven' form of Authentic Leadership Development. It will be of great interest to professionals across a variety of industries who have responsibilities to provide robust leadership development programmes for their organisations, as well as coaches specialising in executive, business and leadership coaching and those interested in new applications for group coaching.

Tony Fusco, DPsych, has pioneered the first evidence-based approach to Authentic Leadership Development in the form of Authentic Leadership Group Coaching. This is a unique and progressive approach to leadership development that is being increasingly adopted within the business community as an effective way to help leaders explore and understand the problems and paradoxes of their own personal leadership experience. In addition to group coaching Authentic Leadership Development, Tony also engages in one-to-one Authentic Leadership coaching in which he helps leaders explore how they can effectively bring more of their genuine self-concept into their role as a leader. This in turn achieves the natural and enduring change that can create paradigm shifts in a leader's performance.

If you would like to find out more about the benefits of Authentic Leadership Group Coaching Dr Tony Fusco can be contacted direct at info@3DLeadership.co.uk

Routledge Focus on Mental Health
Routledge Focus on Mental Health presents short books
on current topics, linking in with cutting-edge research and
practice.

For a full list of titles in this series, please visit www.routledge.com/
Routledge-Focus-on-Mental-Health/book-series/RFMH

Titles in the series:

An Evidence-based Approach to Authentic Leadership Development

Tony Fusco

Routledge
Taylor & Francis Group

LONDON AND NEW YORK

First published 2018
by Routledge

2 Park Square, Milton Park, Abingdon, Oxfordshire OX14 4RN
52 Vanderbilt Avenue, New York, NY 10017

Routledge is an imprint of the Taylor & Francis Group, an informa business

First issued in paperback 2019

British Library Cataloguing in Publication Data
A catalogue record for this book is available from the British Library

Library of Congress Cataloging in Publication Data
Names: Fusco, Tony (Psychologist), author.
Title: An evidence-based approach to authentic leadership development /
Tony Fusco.
Description: Abingdon, Oxon ; New York, NY : Routledge, 2018. |
Identifiers: LCCN 2017050156 (print) | LCCN 2017054835 (ebook) |
ISBN 9781315187990 (Master e-book) | ISBN 9781138732780 (hardback)
Subjects: LCSH: Leadership–Psychological aspects. | Leadership.
Classification: LCC BF637.L4 (ebook) | LCC BF637.L4 F87 2018 (print) |
DDC 158/.4–dc23
LC record available at https://lccn.loc.gov/2017050156

ISBN: 978-1-138-73278-0 (hbk)
ISBN: 978-0-367-33908-1 (pbk)

Typeset in Times New Roman
by Out of House Publishing

To Toni

Contents

Preface

It is said that theories of leadership develop in response to the need of their time. If this is so, then it is no wonder that the idea of Authentic Leadership has become topical over the last 15 years. Since the beginning of the twenty-first century, it seems that one example has followed another in terms of showing us just what bad leadership and poor governance can look like.

Consider Enron's original vision and values statement, which declared: "We treat others as we would like to be treated ourselves... we do not tolerate abusive or disrespectful treatment. Ruthlessness, callousness and arrogance don't belong here." Yet, in 2001, the Enron Corporation collapsed after a lawsuit was filed by investors and an investigation by the US Securities and Exchange Commission led them into bankruptcy, with many top-level employees indicted and given prison sentences.[1] At the Andersen campus, where Arthur Andersen trained new recruits, there was a shrine to ethical accounting;[2] however, as part of their involvement with the former energy giant, they shredded Enron's audit documents during an investigation, attempting to cover up billions in losses at the energy company. The accounting firm was subsequently found guilty of obstructing justice, which put an end to its audit activities in 2002.[3] In the same year, the telecommunications giant, WorldCom, was put into bankruptcy and, at $11 billion, theirs was one of the largest accounting frauds in history at the time. Their former CEO was convicted of orchestrating the fraud and was given a 25-year prison sentence in 2005.[4] More recently, in 2016, there was dieselgate, which saw Europe's biggest car maker, Volkswagen, admit to installing software in diesel engines that was designed to hide their toxic gas emissions.[5] While they were running promotional advertising with Volkswagen engineers dressed as angels, company officials were setting up elaborate systems to lie to customers and to get around pollution controls. Even the world of sport was not immune, as, in 2016, FIFA was plagued by institutional corruption when investigators brought charges against the organisation, accusing FIFA officials of taking millions of dollars in bribes to influence clothing sponsorship contracts, the FIFA presidential election and even the selection process for the World Cup itself.[6]

Political and corporate scandals, of course, are nothing new, but it seems that the recent level and frequency of them has created an appetite for a better form of leadership, one characterised by integrity, trust and a meaningful purpose beyond mere profit. This appetence has prompted both corporate leaders and leadership scholars to look more carefully at the idea of Authentic Leadership. As a result, a wealth of research has since followed (800 research projects as of 2013[7]), which has identified links between Authentic Leadership and a host of organisational benefits, such as employee engagement, productivity, team performance and job satisfaction.[8] What has seemed slow to follow, however, and providing the impetus for this book, is research into the actual development of Authentic Leaders. How do you develop authentic leaders and, crucially, what are the benefits of such development? We now know much about the correlation between increased Authentic Leadership and positive organisational outcomes, but what about the leaders themselves – what does increased authentic leadership mean to them? What are they likely to experience on the inside and what behavioural and performance changes are they likely to witness on the outside as a result of participating in Authentic Leadership Development?

The purpose of this book is to provide evidence-based answers to these questions from several years' research into a group coaching approach to Authentic Leadership Development. It will explain why such a group approach is considered appropriate for Authentic Leadership development and exactly what it can achieve by presenting both statistical and conceptual answers to three core questions about this format of Authentic Leadership Development: does it work? How does it work? And what does 'work' actually mean?

The book offers readers what I believe is the first research and evidence-based approach to Authentic Leadership Development. As such, it is targeted at both leaders and the recruiters and developers of leaders, such as Human Resource (HR), Organisational Development (OD) and Learning & Development (L&D) professionals. My hope is that all professionals with an interest in Authentic Leadership will be able to identify and readily access the information they find most pertinent. However, I don't anticipate this book being of interest to all leaders. There is a type of leader who has the intelligence, insight and answers that enable him/her to deliver their responsibilities effectively and admirably. They know who they are, what they want to achieve with their leadership and exactly how to achieve it. We wish them well. Then, there's another type of leader – maybe just as intelligent, experienced, skilled and successful, but the difference is that these leaders don't just have answers, they also have questions; questions about themselves, their leadership and the connection between the two. These questions may not have been satisfactorily answered, or even asked, in the leadership development experiences they have had to date. If this sounds like you, then you should find this book of interest and relevance.

References

1. www.reference.com/business-finance/enron-s-mission-statement-c6696 fde36f55fbe
2. www.wsj.com/articles/SB1023409436545200
3. http://law.jrank.org/pages/3977/Accounting-Arthur-Andersen-Other-Accounting-Failures.html
4. www.ecommercetimes.com/story/45542.html
5. http://fortune.com/2015/09/27/volkswagen-staff-warned-scandal-
6. www.inc.com/will-yakowicz/biggest-big-business-fails-of-2015.html
7. Ladkin, D. & Spiller, C. (Eds.) (2013). *Authentic Leadership: Clashes, Convergences and Coalescences*. Cheltenham, UK: Edward Elgar Publishing.
8. Gardner, W. L., Cogliser, C. C., Davis, K. M. & Dickens, M. P. (2011). *Authentic leadership: a review of the literature and research agenda*. The Leadership Quarterly, *22*, 1120–1145.

Introduction

Tony Fusco

Peruse any leadership reading list and you will find an ever-growing selection of titles on Authentic Leadership. Business CEO and Harvard professor, Bill George, led the way in 2003 with *Authentic Leadership: Rediscovering the Secrets to Creating Lasting Value*,[1] containing the inspiring chapter headings one would expect from such a luminary establishment as Harvard (e.g. "Missions Motivate, Dollars Don't"; "Acquisitions Aren't Just About Money"; "Shareholders Come Third"; "It's the Customer Stupid!"). George's follow-up book, *True North: Discover Your Authentic Leadership*,[2] was published in 2007 and started to get a bit more personal, with chapter titles such as "Practicing Your Values and Principles," "Leadership with Purpose and Passion" and "What Motivates You to Be a Leader?" Another Harvard book in this field was the 2006 *Why Should Anyone Be Led by You? What It Takes to Be an Authentic Leader*[3] by Rob Goffee and Gareth Jones of the London School of Economics (LSE) and Instituto de Empresa (IE) business schools. Their advice on the subject is implied in their choice of chapter headings: "Be Yourself – More – with Skill," "Know and Show Yourself – Enough," "Communicate – with Care" and "Remain Authentic – but Conform Enough." These book titles were all hugely successful and set the scene for the business readerships' first foray into the newly emerging field of Authentic Leadership. There have been over a dozen books following on from these first texts on Authentic Leadership, but all offered pretty much only a variation on a theme. First, they offer the inspiring tales of different leaders' journeys and how they came to be as successful as they are. These are always entertaining, but I for one have difficulty moving them from the 'entertainment' category to the 'useful' category. Second, they offer direct advice on how to be and lead authentically. Their advice ranges from the common stock – *discover your purpose and create your vison* or *clarify your principles and articulate your values* – to the somewhat ephemeral – *care daily for the Soul* and *manage human hungers* – to the frankly banal – *pay Attention and learn from failure!* The final offering many of these books make is in the form of Authentic Leadership Worksheets. These exercises are designed to help you delve into some of your deepest recesses and magically uncover your strengths and weaknesses, choose from a list of values, set some life goals and sort out your work–life balance – Authentic Leadership 101 complete!

If I'm sounding somewhat sceptical of these approaches, it's because I am. I'm not discounting their entertainment value and I'm sure they're useful in stimulating reflection on long plane and train journeys, but I can't help wonder how looking passively at a list of preordained values can really help me understand my own – they're notoriously difficult things to identify and understand at the best of times. Can I really establish the purpose of my life and leadership simply because the question is written down on a page in front of me? If it were that simple, wouldn't I have worked it out for myself already?

Authentic Leadership is a laudable goal, both logically and intuitively. But the fundamental thing missing in the entire Authentic Leadership field, in my opinion, is the answer to one key question: *how* do we develop Authentic Leaders? The scholarly literature is awash with outcome studies that clearly illustrate the correlation between Authentic Leadership and various positive employee and organisational outcomes – engagement, commitment, productivity, well-being, etc. – but even in the world of academic research and publication there remains a conspicuous absence of research studies into how we actually develop Authentic Leaders. There is a handful of papers that put forward case study data and some related theoretical propositions, but so far there has been no robust science underlying the whole concept of Authentic Leadership Development.

That is what I believe differentiates this book from other texts on Authentic Leadership. For the first time, I believe, this book offers an empirically developed and evidenced approach to Authentic Leadership Development in the form of Authentic Leadership Group Coaching. Throughout the book, I shall introduce this new approach to ALD and, in the process, address three core questions: does it work? How does it work? And what does 'work' actually mean? This will be done in a manner that I hope effectively straddles a balance between theory and practice. My overall aim is to offer sufficient detail to assure the reader of the sound theoretical underpinnings of this group approach, while also clearly demonstrating its output and associated benefits. While the assessment of this form of ALD is based soundly on a scientific approach, authenticity is itself something of a philosophical idea and ideal. So, while each reader may have a leaning more towards one of these perspectives than the other, I hope to bring them together in a way each reader will find both interesting and useful.

To that end, in Chapter 1, we shall consider the existential nature of authenticity and how its philosophic roots informed and shaped the group coaching format presented here, before moving on to discuss the three questions mentioned above. Readers, of course, are at liberty to skip this section, perhaps thinking philosophy has no relevance to them in their modern working life, though I would propose to you that if you are interested in developing yourself as an Authentic Leader, on some level you are also interested in the questions that existential philosophy pose, questions around self, purpose, values and meaning. In addition, and perhaps on a more immediate note, it will help you to understand why the ALD programme described in this book is designed as it is and achieves what it does. For this purpose, I shall offer a *very* brief overview of existential philosophy and the contributions that I consider particularly relevant to authenticity and Authentic Leadership Development. This, I trust, will give you, the reader, a sound understanding of the subject that can be carried throughout the rest of the book as you explore what authenticity and Authentic Leadership might mean personally to you.

Chapter 2 examines and answers the following question: does it work? Here, we consider the instruments currently being used to assess Authentic Leadership, their uses, their limitations and the results of using these within the research presented here. Scores on these instruments were statistically significant, both in level of probability and effect size, appearing to answer the first question in the affirmative and that yes, group coaching does work as an effective form of Authentic Leadership Development. However, there is growing controversy over the design and use of these instruments, with some arguing that they reduce the concept of Authentic Leadership to a leadership competency framework (i.e. if you're x and y, then you're authentic in your leadership and if you're not x and y, then you're not authentic in your leadership). This will be discussed, as will the fact that the current rationalist approach generally in the field conspicuously ignores the philosophic roots of the authenticity concept.

Chapters 3 and 4 examine and answer the following question: how does it work? In the process, they bring together social and self-psychology to help identify and isolate exactly how and why this form of ALD works. This second question will be answered statistically, conceptually and anecdotally with the inclusion of participant accounts, who give their views on the group experience and how it has helped them in their leadership roles.

The final question, of course, is another that most, if not all, leaders will want to know the answer to: what does 'work' actually mean? What is the impact of Authentic Leadership Development at a business and organisational level? Chapter 5 examines and answers this question. In this chapter, I shall set out exactly what the leadership and organisational benefits are that can be expected from the group coaching approach to ALD. For example, is Authentic Leadership just about ethics and knowing your values or is it about something more? The research demonstrates that it is indeed about more... much more. It turns out that Authentic Leadership is not just about ethical leadership (which itself comes under scrutiny and question) – it's also about proactive, purposeful and strategic leadership. It is about the selection of goals concordant with the leader's self-concept. It's also not just about understanding yourself – it's also about understanding others. And it's about leadership confidence and clarity. As demonstrable return on investment is a perennial and difficult issue within organisational L&D, an important aim of this book is also to clearly demonstrate the organisational benefits of ALD. In the process, the hope is that this book will offer the insight and confidence to all those involved in both leadership and leadership development that genuine ALD is both achievable and worthwhile.

Chapter 6 explores the place of values, morals and ethics in Authentic Leadership. This is a much-debated issue. Many researchers and practitioners believe that authentic leadership should be based on ethical leadership and/or a high moral cause. Whilst I believe an understanding of and congruence with personal values are key aspects of Authentic Leadership, I propose that being a beacon of morals and ethics is not. This research and that of others demonstrate that an Authentic Leader can be true to themselves and their aspirations and pursue personally meaningful goals, yet not have a particular focus on ethical practice or a moral crusade. I also highlight the fact that as theories of ethical and moral leadership already exist independently in the field – they don't need to be shoehorned into a theory of Authentic Leadership, particularly if the empirical evidence isn't there in support.

Chapter 7 considers the issue of evaluation and how appropriate it is or is not for Authentic Leadership Development. We look at what the Return on Investment (ROI) Institute considers best practice in leadership development evaluation and where the concepts of programme objectives, competency frameworks and evaluation fit within ALD. This chapter shows how evaluation can be achieved up to a performance improvement level, but how the difference between tangible and intangible organisational benefits then makes the idea of return on investment not a germane one.

A final point to make is about the science underpinning the ALD approach presented here. A judgement has been made that it is important to let the reader be privy to just what that underpinning research and development (R&D) entailed, which brings an obvious tension. I want to demonstrate the science to those who are interested while not distracting those who are not. To try and achieve this, I shall make top-level references to the scientific process where relevant, but endeavour to do so in a manner that won't interrupt the flow of the overall message. Hopefully, this will be achieved to the satisfaction of each section of readership.

Similarly, each of our three guiding questions will probably be of more or less interest to the different readers of the book. For example, any one in a procurement role may want to be assured of the answer to question 1 – does it work? If I brought this form of leadership development into my company, am I investing effectively? Potential participants and company owners may be more concerned with question 3 – what does 'work' actually mean? What tangible difference will it make to me and/or my leadership team and their performance? How ultimately will it benefit the business? And question 2 may be of interest to potential practitioners, coaches and group facilitators who are keen to understand exactly what works and how and why.

I am mindful of the perils of writing something that is trying to be many things to many people and, in the end, the respective readers will be the judges of whether I have succeeded in navigating these perils. Nevertheless, it may still be helpful to provide a quick rationale of my approach in each of the following chapters. In answering question 1, I have included some statistical evidence because I can think of no better way of addressing this first question conclusively. The instruments used were the ALQ and the ALI and, for those unfamiliar with statistics, I shall explain what the analysis means in very straightforward terms. For question 2, I have included the first part of the qualitative research method I used called Grounded Theory. This is a rather painstaking method that breaks down the entire contents of participant's reports and interviews and codes the data, themes it and finally categorises it into a conceptually sound explanatory framework illustrating what is going on throughout the process. This section gets a little involved, as I also introduce another quantitative measure that assesses the individual leader's self-concept clarity. So this is a mixed research methods section, but hopefully I've succeeded in making it a clear and relatively painless one. For question 3, we pick up Grounded Theory again to identify and demonstrate what qualities are developed through this ALD approach and taken back into the workplace; that is, what does Authentic Leadership Group Coaching achieve for the participants and their respective organisations?

References

1. George, B. (2003). *Authentic Leadership: Rediscovering the Secrets to Creating Lasting Value*. San Francisco: John Wiley & Sons, Jossey-Bass.
2. George, B. (2010). *True North: Discover Your Authentic Leadership* (Vol. 143). San Francisco: John Wiley & Sons, Jossey-Bass.
3. Goffee, R. & Jones, G. (2006). *Why Should Anyone Be Led by You? What It Takes to Be an Authentic Leader*. Boston, MA: Harvard Business Press.

1   A brief history of authenticity

In his book *In Search of Authenticity*,[1] Jacob Golomb dramatically describes the concept of authenticity as "a protest against the blind, mechanical acceptance of an externally imposed code of values" (p.11) and that "we create our authenticity; it is not delivered to us by higher authorities" (p.25). He is suggesting that authenticity is about matching up to some form of internal standard and living in accord with that individually chosen meaning. In this way, authentic people create an individual purpose and direction for their lives that can't be understood purely in terms of external meaning or purpose. One particular meaning or purpose can never be objectively right or wrong if it represents accurately who we are: it can only ever be subjectively measured and determined by our own internal standard. The cosmos can never justify one way as right over another – only we can judge that, but by the same token, being authentic means you have to take full responsibility for these choices and decisions. For this reason alone, it is perhaps understandable why some people struggle with the uncertainty and angst this can create and prefer to shelter within the values and norms of an existing cultural, political, social or religious system that can offer them the warmth and security of a *human huddle*. However, if as an individual I can tolerate this slight chill of uncertainty, I am rewarded with a self-mastery that means I am in control of both myself and my life and am able to give to both a coherent sense of direction and purpose. So, authenticity is not judged by specifically *what* I do, but more *how and why* I choose to do what I do. Ultimately, to be authentic, these decisions must be made autonomously. It is therefore not surprising these terms have a very similar meaning in early Greek. *Authentes* means to 'act on one's own authority' and *autonomos* meaning 'self-rule'. We begin in the realm of Ancient Greece to start a very brief historical account of the philosophic roots of authenticity and then continue by moving through two further ages and perspectives of existentialism and post-modern philosophy.

Ancient Greece

Know thyself! This is possibly the ancient Greeks' most famous maxim and is inscribed above the entrance to the Temple of Apollo at Delphi. Delphi was considered the centre of the ancient classical world and was the seat of the all-knowing and all-seeing Oracle around 500 to 300 BC.[2] The Oracle was considered the font of all knowledge and was believed to prophesise while possessed by the god Apollo himself. Such was the Oracle's influence that she was consulted on all important decisions that affected the Greek world, including war and colonisation.[3] A common misconception is that this famous command to *know thyself* originated with the philosopher Socrates and although he is said to have embodied it, referring to it in various discourses and dialogues, it was in a bid to follow the established wisdom of the original inscription that Socrates himself became known as a man who "in his character, his conduct and his opinions, there are no contradictions" (p.53).[4] Fast forward 2000 years and the influence of Socrates is still keenly felt, as is philosophy's concern with the quest to both *know thyself* and *be thyself*, particularly in a branch of philosophy known as existentialism.

Existentialism

Existential philosophy concerns itself with the fundamentals of human existence such as individual freedom, responsibility, choice, meaning, purpose and authenticity.[5] There are numerous great thinkers whose work may be considered existential in nature, but in this brief review we will look at just three central figures: Søren Kierkegaard, Friedrich Nietzsche and Martin Heidegger.

It is the Dane, Søren Kierkegaard (1813–1855), who is generally considered the founder of existential philosophy. He focused most of his work on ethics, morality and the psychology and philosophy of religion. He was a great thinker, but also applied his philosophy to his way of life, believing that the creation of an authentic life was nothing short of an *existential vocation*. As such, his overriding concern was with personal choice and commitment in how to live one's life as an individual, stating, "The thing is to find a truth that is true for me, to find the idea for which I can live and die" (p.15).[6] Kierkegaard was deeply influenced by Socrates and praised the Greek for being the first to study with *decisive force* the concept of the *existing individual*.[7] And like Socrates he believed true knowledge began with self knowledge. As well as on thought, there was also an influence on style. Much like Socrates, Kierkegaard wasn't prone to direct instruction or lecturing. He preferred a more indirect form of communicating, allowing the reader to learn their own lessons through personal descriptions of his own life views.[8] He often did not conclude anything at all, rather just illuminating all sides of the prism, in much the same way that Socrates did by using questioning as his primary tool of enquiry. To this day, 'Socratic questioning' is a term and technique used extensively by coaches to help leaders and others explore and pursue their own personally significant lines of enquiry. This method of non-prescriptive and vicarious social learning is a technique at the heart of the coaching approach to Authentic Leadership Development described here. After all, no one can *teach* you directly how to be an authentic leader, but they *can* help you learn.

Friedrich Nietzsche (1844–1900) was a towering German philosopher, appointed as a professor at Basel University before even receiving his doctorate at age 24.[9] Like Kierkegaard, he was also influenced by the Ancient Greeks, but found the pre-Socratics more to his liking. Also like Kierkegaard, he was a *passionate individualist* and had only distain for the *herd*. He tended to use the term 'individuality' more than 'authenticity'. He believed engaging with the world as an individual was life's most important task and that we should give expression to life through our own unique perspectives and purposes. He said that when you achieve this, you are in control and you *become what you already are*. In true existential fashion, Nietzsche believed that there was no one objectively right way or truth to life and that each individual has to understand the world through his or her own perspective. He believed there were no facts only interpretations. When his famous fictional character, Zarathustra,[10] was pressed by devotees to tell them *the way*, he simply replied, "This is my way... what is yours... for the way – that does not exist" (p.307).[11] Being authentic means defining yourself and making conscious choices about your life that accurately represent that ongoing uniqueness. Another of Nietzsche's pertinent ideas reflecting this is that we are continually in flux and as we are exposed to more experience of life, so we must continually examine our thoughts and perspectives. He stresses that we must continually reappraise and rethink our understanding of ourselves and our world to ensure they remain a true expression of who we authentically are – not to sleepwalk, but to move consciously through life. The purpose of this *self-overcoming*, as Nietzsche termed it, is to achieve maturity, authenticity and profound self-knowledge and to be "… the free author of one's own self" (p.70).[1] Such insights led none other than Sigmund Freud to exclaim, "He had a more penetrating knowledge of himself than any other man who ever lived or was ever likely to live" (p.20).[12]

Martin Heidegger (1889–1976) was another highly significant German philosopher who was influenced by both Kierkegaard and Nietzsche and was Professor of Philosophy at both Marburg and Freiburg universities.[9] Perhaps the most relevant aspect of Heidegger's philosophy with regards to the ALD approach described here is his focus on temporality and the belief that to live authentically as an integrated individual, you need to have a unifying perspective of your past, your present and your future. The usual concept of time sees time as disconnected and as something external to you that you simply travel through. However, the existential view is that your existence spreads across time and that it isn't just the present that has significance, but the past, present and future all join together in a meaningful flow. The past is alive and well and constantly informing your present and future in terms of who you are now and who you'll become in the future. Heidegger says that we are projected forward towards future possibilities from the experience of our present shaped by our past and that these coalesce to make our present actions and future goals relevant and meaningful. In this way, living authentically means all three domains need to be connected across time in a meaningful way. Heidegger believed that the future was of particular importance when trying to live as an authentic being because we are always reaching ahead of ourselves towards future possibilities in a self-defining way. However, this forward directedness also makes us aware of our finitude and that our lives are bounded on both sides by birth and death. For Heidegger, as for all existentialists, acceptance of our finitude is key to living an authentic life, as it gives all of our choices and decisions in the present a profound significance and calls upon us to engage with life in an active and resolute way, committed to what we have decided is personally meaningful. In this way, we answer what he describes as an almost primordial search for authenticity: "I first hear a call to be authentic. I owe it to myself to own myself. I feel responsible and, in response, attempt to satisfy this call" (p.314).[13] It is nothing short of *winning self-possession.*[1]

Modernity and authenticity

In addition to these three central figures, there is the work of many others that beckon in any introduction to the concept of authenticity, such as the literature of the French existentialists Sartre and Camus, the existential psychiatry of Binswanger and Jaspers, the humanistic psychology of Fromm, Maslow, Rogers and Erikson and the philosophic psychotherapy of Frankl, May and Yalom. Although the works of these and others are all fascinating in their own right, they are well beyond the scope of this short overview. So, I shall just include a small selection of contemporary individuals who I think are important for this introduction inasmuch as they bring us right up to date – individuals who also foretoken some of the challenges to personal authenticity that we might all come to face in a not-too-distant future.

In *The Malaise of Modernity*, social theorist, Professor Charles Taylor, echoes the words of all of these earlier thinkers and warns us that if we fail to find the design of our own life, we miss the point of our life:

> There is a certain way of being human that is my way. I am called upon to live my life in this way, and not in imitation of anyone else's. But this gives a new importance to being true to myself. If I am not, I miss the point of my life, I miss what being human is for me.
>
> (pp.28–29)[14]

In this book, Taylor emphasises the point that when we create the unique design of our lives, we do so in a constant battle with the pressures of the modern external world, a world that incessantly tries to shape and conform us to its own design. On a similar theme, political scientist, Professor Anthony Giddens, in *Modernity and Self-Identity*,[15] talks about a reality inversion that can occur when the familiarity generated by the constant exposure to virtual images and experiences results in the real objects and events being somehow less real when actually encountered. Consider the neuroscientist, Professor Susan Greenfield's, tale of a friend's young daughter who, upon encountering a large jellyfish on the beach, exclaimed, "Wow… isn't it realistic!"[16]

In *The Saturated Self*, Professor Kenneth Gergen also forewarns of the problems for humanity's search for authenticity in post-modern times. He introduces several prophetic terms that increasingly relate to the concept of authenticity in the modern world. For example, he coined the phrase *technologies of social saturation*, which relates to the things that immerse us ever deeper into the socially connected world and expose us to endless images and opinions of others. This increased *populating of the self* can lead us to experience a *vertigo of unlimited multiplicity* – a *multiphrenia* – that, in time, could even lead to the *erasure of the individual self*. It is sobering to consider he wrote this when the worst offenders were probably Sky TV and MTV, sometime before the whole force of the wired world and social media was unleashed. Gergen prophesied:

> Emerging technologies saturate us with the voices of humankind. As we absorb their varied rhymes and reasons, they become part of us and we of them. Social saturation furnishes us with a multiplicity of incoherent and unrelated languages of the self. This fragmentation of self-conceptions corresponds to a multiplicity of incoherent and disconnected relationships. These relationships pull us in myriad directions... the very concept of an authentic self... recedes from view. The fully saturated self becomes no self at all.
>
> (pp.6–7)[17]

If this sounds like far-fetched futurology, reflect on what Susan Greenfield says on the subject. Baroness Greenfield is Professor of Synaptic Pharmacology at Oxford University and Director of the Institute for the Future of the Mind. As one of Britain's leading neuroscientists, Professor Greenfield focuses her research on how the brain gives rise to a sense of consciousness and, in particular, what our world of rapid change means for the human brain and for human nature. In her book *ID: The Quest for Meaning in the 21st Century*, Greenfield proposes that "our identity as twenty-first-century individuals is in crisis" (p.117).[16] She believes that the inner-sanctum of the individual self is under threat in post-modern life through the erosion of what she calls the *firewall* between our inner and outer lives. She makes the point that the brain, hence the mind, hence the self, is *inextricably interlinked in dialogue* with the outside world. The increasingly pervasive and interlinked technologies of info-technology, nano-technology and bio-technology could lead to a culture that in turn has the capacity to dismantle traditional means of individual demarcation and thus *obliterate the individual* altogether. It was disconcerting to hear Gergen talk in the late twentieth century about the sense of self "fraying around the edges" and warning that "it is the achievement of authenticity that the technologies of social saturation serve to prevent" (p.203).[17] It is even more unsettling to hear Greenfield talk in the early twenty-first century, not of the self receding or fraying, but of its inevitable *obliteration* – potentially by mid-century.

Sufficiently real is this anticipated impact of technology on our identities and sense of self that it prompted a UK Government report from the Office for Science entitled *Future Identities* in 2013.[18] Professor Sir John Beddington, Chief Government Scientific Advisor, says in the executive summary:

The report discusses an emerging trend towards 'hyper-connectivity', where mobile technology and the ubiquity of the internet enable people to be constantly connected across many different platforms. Hyper-connectivity is already removing any meaningful distinction between online and offline identities, while also blurring 'public' and 'private' identities. The trend could also act to increase the pace of change, leading to more dynamic and changeable identities.

(p.3)

Even if this impact of post-modern life on the self doesn't quite follow the trajectory Professor Greenfield predicts, she nonetheless concludes emphatically in *The Neuroscience of Identity* that if as a species our most basic and valuable talent is a highly sensitive adaptability to our environment, then screen-based life with prolonged surfing, virtual reality gaming and social-networking cannot fail to have a transformational effect on our mental states and the eventual consciousness of the human species.[19] So, even if the degree and timescale are yet to be fully determined, this suggests that the challenges of personal identity and authenticity will only increase for progressive generations to come.

References

1. Golomb, J. (1995). *In Search of Authenticity: From Kierkegaard to Camus.* London: Routledge.
2. Russell, B. (1961). *The History of Western Philosophy.* London: George Allen & Unwin Ltd.
3. Graves, R. (1955). *The Greek Myths.* Harmondsworth: Penguin Books.
4. Warner. R. (1958). *The Greek Philosophers.* New York: New American Library.
5. Nauman, St E. (1972). *The New Dictionary of Existentialism.* New Jersey: The Citadel Press.
6. Dru, A. (1938). *The Journals of Soren Kierkegaard.* London: Oxford University Press.
7. Gardiner, P. (1988). *Kierkegaard: A Very Short Introduction.* Oxford: Oxford University Press.
8. Ferguson, R. (2013). *Life Lessons from Kierkegaard.* London: Macmillan.
9. Blackham, H. J. (1952). *Six Existential Thinkers.* London: Routledge & Keegan Paul Ltd.
10. Nietzsche, F. (1954). *Thus Spoke Zarathustra.* Trans. W. Kaufmann. New York: Viking.
11. Solomon, R. (1974). *Existentialism.* New York: Random House.

12. Kaufman, W. (1975). *Existentialism: From Dostoevsky to Sartre*. New York: Penguin.
13. Heidegger, M. (1962). *Being and Time*. Trans. J. Macquarrie & E. Robinson. New York: Harper Row.
14. Taylor, C. (1996). *The Malaise of Modernity*. Ontario: Anansi Press.
15. Giddens, A. (1991). *Modernity and Self-Identity*. Cambridge: Polity Press.
16. Greenfield, S. (2008). *ID: The Quest for Meaning in the 21st Century*. London: Sceptre – Hodder & Stoughton Ltd.
17. Gergen, K. (1991). *The Saturated Self*. New York: Basic Books.
18. www.gov.uk/government/uploads/system/uploads/attachment_data/file/273966/13-523-future-identities-changing-identities-report.pdf
19. Greenfield, S. (2011). *You and Me: The Neuroscience of Identity*. London: Notting Hill Editions Ltd.

2 Does Authentic Leadership Group Coaching work?

We have taken a brief historical tour of humanity's interest in the concept of authenticity, so let's now quickly look at where we are in terms of the modern scientific concept of authenticity. This will also give us the background to the instruments used in this section. In 2003, research psychologist Michael Kernis[1] hypothesised four components of authenticity: awareness, unbiased processing, action and relational orientation. This model was then further refined and developed in 2005[2] and again in 2008[3] by other researchers who offered their own slightly adapted models of Authentic Leadership (AL) to include: self-awareness, balanced processing, internalised moral perspective and relational transparency. These researchers then constructed a measurement instrument around these four components called the Authentic Leadership Questionnaire (ALQ)[3] and a further developed version, the Authentic Leadership Inventory (ALI).[4] Although these instruments are not without their critics, which we shall come on to, the most straightforward way to 'technically' assess the efficacy of the AL group coaching approach was to use these two 'validated' Authentic Leadership instruments.

The ALQ is based on the multidimensional model of the Authentic Leadership construct outlined above and is a 16-item, 5-point scale that has internal consistency reliability for each of its four scales: self-awareness, relational transparency, internalised moral perspective and balanced processing. The ALI is a 14-item, 5-point scale based on the same theoretical framework and dimensions as the ALQ and also has content validity, reliability and internal consistency. Both assessment questionnaires were completed by each leader who participated in the research described here at the beginning of day 1 and at the end of day 3, three months later.

T-tests

To establish if the pre- and post-coaching Authentic Leadership scores were significantly different, a repeated measures *t*-test was performed. In simple terms, *t*-tests are used to establish the reliable difference between two sets of scores; in this instance, the difference between the leaders' average scores before and after they participated in the AL group coaching. Why not just look at the average score differences? Well, that would tell us whether they are different, but not whether they are *reliably* different. *T*-tests give us inferential statistics, meaning they don't just tell us about our existing population of ALD participants; rather, they enable us to infer or predict the scores of leaders beyond our existing sample who have not yet participated. That is the power of inferential statistics over simple descriptive statistics such as averages, medians, etc. Both sets of scores showed statistical significance, as illustrated in Table 2.1 and Table 2.2.

The ALQ shows significance at $t = 2.83$, $p<0.01$ and the ALI at $t = 3.84$, $p<0.001$. The *p*-value is the probability that the difference between the scores of our participants could be produced by random (i.e. is the difference *real?*). The usual cut-off point for statistical significance is 5 per cent or $p = 0.05$. This means there is a 5 per cent chance that the same score difference could have been achieved by chance and therefore a 95 per cent probability it was achieved as a result of the intervention under investigation. For both the ALQ and the ALI, there are *p*-values of <0.01 and <0.001 indicating 1 per cent and a 0.1 per cent probabilities, respectively, that our participant's scores were achieved by random chance. This indicates a 99 per cent probability that the ALQ scores and a 99.9 per cent chance that the ALI scores were achieved as

Table 2.1 ALQ and ALI – paired sample *t*-tests

Authentic Leadership measures	Mean difference	Standard deviation	t	df	Significance (two-tailed)
ALQ	2.68	4.72	2.837	24	0.01
ALI	3.64	4.73	3.845	24	0.001

Table 2.2 Pre- and post-coaching ALQ and ALI mean and standard deviation scores

Authentic Leadership measure	Pre-coaching		Post-coaching	
	Mean	Standard deviation	Mean	Standard deviation
ALQ total score	48.20	5.82	50.88	5.56
ALI total score	52.76	4.93	56.40	4.33

a result of the coaching intervention, meaning there is a 99.9 per cent probability that AL group coaching *works*!

As both sets of scores showed statistical significance, something called the Cohen d effect size was then calculated, which showed a score for the ALQ of $d = 0.57$ and for the ALI of $d = 0.77$. Whereas the p-value measures the reliability of difference in the scores, the d-value measures the magnitude of this difference. Above $d = 0.50$ indicates that the average person undergoing AL group coaching would perform better on their scores than 69 per cent of a control group who didn't go through the group coaching. At $d = 0.80$, that rises to 79 per cent. This is somewhat hypothetical, as we didn't use a control group, but it is an indication of the potential power of the AL group coaching process. It is also worth noting that the individual components making up the overall Authentic Leadership construct were also analysed and seven out of eight of the score increases across both instruments, were also statistically significant.

There are some limitations to the t-test and one is that you can only generalise to similar populations. For example, if it were a clinical drugs trial testing adults for cholesterol levels, you could only generalise such results to other adults and not to children. Therefore, this is a suitable test for our evaluation because we are only interested in purposive sampling, generalising from an existing sample of suitable leaders motivated to participate in AL group coaching to a broader but similar population of leaders but not for example, to an unsuitable or unmotivated population of leaders. Or those who fail to meet other purposive sampling criteria for an AL coaching group.

Trouble ahead for Authentic Leadership measurement

As alluded to earlier, there is a fundamental issue currently under discussion in the Authentic Leadership literature concerning the nature of authenticity itself and whether it can in any way be construed and measured in behavioural terms. Simply put, is there a list of skills or traits, such as those included in these instruments, that identifies the authentic leader? The issue with this, as some readers may already be sensing, is that this, in effect, offers us an Authentic Leader competency framework. If you *are* these things, then you are authentic, and if you're not... well, then you're not!

Consider the usual names that come to mind when thinking about Authentic Leaders: Mahatma Gandhi, Nelson Mandela, Martin Luther King, etc. – all incredible individuals who used themselves as instruments for social change. Now add to that list modern-day philanthropic leaders such as Warren Bennis and Bill Gates. These are all leaders who have demonstrated principled and purposeful leadership in their philanthropic activities. Yet all are different – different in personal history, style, motivation and aspiration. And that is the point of authenticity: it is neither preordained nor predetermined. It is something profoundly personal and deeply rooted within each individual. And yet, the scholarly field of Authentic Leadership has, almost inevitably, tried to define it, conceptualise it and measure it. The motivation is understandable. After so many global examples of poor corporate and political intendancy, the field sought an antidote and concluded Authentic Leadership was the answer. However, it did so in a predictably deterministic and positivistic manner, with little or no consideration of what allied fields such as philosophy had to say about a subject that it had been debating for centuries. A recent paper on the subject titled 'Theorising leadership authenticity'[5] summarises this: "Whilst the number of articles discussing authenticity in relation to leadership may be increasing, few overtly relate the concept to philosophical foundations… [or offer any] convincing ontological basis for the concept of authenticity as it is applied to leadership" (p.327). Other theorists[6] also criticise the focus on leader traits and behaviours and make the point that phenomenological views of Authentic Leadership are all but absent, reflecting a deterministic view of authenticity that contrasts markedly with the idea of authenticity espoused by philosophers.

There is growing criticism of the developing orthodoxy of Authentic Leadership research being based upon an empirical and realist epistemology that almost certainly limits the scope for the development of the Authentic Leadership concept. Critics argue that the aim of this approach is to "identify and define the core characteristics of a universal model of leadership" (p.331).[5] Ultimately, concerned with a quantifiable and generalised theory of Authentic Leadership that will "restrict our potential understanding of authenticity in relation to leadership" (p.331).[5] Other authors concur[7] that "in its haste to be operationalised, the concept of authenticity as it is currently used in authentic leadership is limited" (p.118), with many agreeing that Authentic Leadership as it is currently theorised needs to move away from prescriptions of how leaders should behave so as to genuinely enable each leader's own unique approach to emerge.

All of these authors, theorists and researchers agree that the existential perspective has something important to offer the study of leadership precisely because it goes beyond the traditional and limited rationalistic-objectivist approach. It can deepen our understanding of leadership as it focuses more on *individual leadership* rather than on *abstract leadership*, and in so doing can "provide a deeper understanding of the human experience which has long been ignored in leadership theory. If AL theory embraces its existential roots… a substantial contribution to leadership theory can be made" (p.126).[7] It is the purpose of the Authentic Leadership Development described in this book to provide this first point in a bid to achieve the second.

Existential leadership development

Considering the above, it becomes clear that Authentic Leadership cannot be taught. It is not based upon a fixed set of behaviours or traits. It can only be achieved through the exploration of the deep human issues that make up the unique human condition, such as an individual's personal beliefs, values and purpose. This is in contrast to the usual acquisition of conceptual knowledge and concrete skills that most leadership development interventions teach. Authenticity in leadership cannot be taught in such a straightforward manner, as "the concept of authenticity goes to the heart of what it is to be human and hence dwelling on 'what it is to be authentically human' before asking 'what is it to be an authentic leader' seems... essential" (p.122).[7] So, how in a leadership development programme does one ask and answer the questions: what is it to be an authentic human, what is it to be an Authentic Leader and how do we develop each of these?

I propose an answer in the form of an existentially orientated approach to leadership development. If authenticity is a fundamentally existential issue, then it follows that the development of authenticity must be existentially informed. It is also phenomenological in nature and not scientific. The world of organisational leadership is a complex one and therefore it is understandable that the field should be drawn towards answers that offer clarity and order through the complexity and disorder of the modern world. However, as we've seen above and as we probably intuitively know, authenticity cannot be compartmentalised, measured, predicted and controlled. A theory or model of great leadership has forever eluded researchers, but when we see great leadership, it is apparent it comes down to deep-rooted authenticity. Richard Branson was not born of a competency framework, nor were Steve Jobs or Jack Welch. Their great leadership and that of countless other effective leaders comes from within, from an enduring, principled and purposeful leadership executed genuinely, unwaveringly and authentically.

Past–present–future approach to Authentic Leadership Group Coaching

Business, political and military leadership biographies often show how an individual's North Star,[8] the guiding light of their life's purpose and meaning, is formed and developed in relation to what they have learnt to value. The Authentic Leadership Development programme presented in this book is based on a past–present–future group coaching approach that helps leaders clarify what is of true value to them, personally and professionally. It does this by indirectly tackling the issue of authenticity by focusing leaders on the issues that lie at the heart of authenticity, such as personal values, meaning and responsibility. Looking at leadership through such a lens brings a leader clarity on what is important to them, what they stand for, what they will not stand for and what they ultimately want to achieve with their leadership. Pondering issues of such magnitude along a temporal perspective of past, present and future brings forth tremendous clarity and deliberate self-determination. Below, I will briefly outline what such a past–present–future programme looks like.

The past

Day 1 of this approach to Authentic Leadership Group Coaching asks leaders to look back over the significant events in their lives and to make sense of how these have influenced who they have become as a person and a leader. It invites leaders to reflect on their past in an attempt to understand how and where their key life lessons were formed and how these in turn inform their leadership principles and purpose. The process of mapping out one's life trajectory seldom fails to present the individual with often unexpected self-insight and understanding. As well as aiding clarity on values and personal meaning, this exercise brings into focus two other fundamental personal concerns of temporality and finitude and that, being self-conscious creatures, humans are uniquely aware of the passage of time. These are subjects of too grand a magnitude for many leadership development programmes perhaps, but when exploring personal authenticity, the thought of our transience can be a great values clarifier.[9] The conscious appreciation of our temporality and ultimate finitude can make us realise that our lives are not automatically underwritten by significance or meaning and that we should accept responsibility and consciously choose what it is we value and want to achieve with our lives and our leadership.

The present

Day 2 relates to a leader's relationships with others as they exist in the cultural and organisational networks within which they are embedded. Authentic Leadership Group Coaching brings the participants' social world right into the here and now of the group, as each leader relates individually and collectively with the other group members, engaging with them in much the same way as they do with significant others in their outer worlds. The work that can happen in this context, in terms of observational feedback, questioning and challenging, is already a well-known therapeutic factor in group therapy. Its relevance for group coaching and in particular Authentic Leadership Group Coaching is now also becoming apparent.[10,11] As will be discussed in more depth later, this focus on the leaders' relations with others also acts as a direct window into their relationship with their own leadership identity.

The future

Day 3 brings together all that has personal significance for the leader and, by drawing together all of their ideals, values and principles, they achieve an overall sense of authentic meaning, purpose and desired-for future. The existentialist view is that authentic individuals should be self-determining and should create their own personal meaning and purpose, giving expression to their *autonomous self-rule* mentioned in the Introduction. However, as part of a wider organisational community, some leaders have more of an opportunity to do this than others. There is an inherent complexity of life within the organisation. Autonomy and self-determination will inevitably have to compromise to at least some degree with the need for direction and coordination. However, "Authenticity involves a connection to, and expression of, a higher aspiration or purpose" (p.128).[7] So, the future perspective invites leaders to ponder an elevated purpose and a yet-to-be-built future that might have personal significance for them. Such an existential perspective bids each individual to face and accept responsibility for their own lives and careers and to choose what in their lives and their leadership holds genuine value and meaning. It means making choices and accepting responsibility for these choices and the purpose they imbue into their personal existence.

In conclusion, the tradition of leadership research to date has generally been one of a *rationalist paradigm*. In the past, the primary focus of leadership research has been an attempt to distil down the essence of leadership to identify *composite qualities, behaviours and competencies* (p.409).[12] The ultimate aim of this has been to seek objectivity, generalisability and, ultimately, predictability and control. In this respect, an existential and phenomenological approach to Authentic Leadership Development as presented in this book is set aside from most other forms of leadership development. Rather than attempting to standardise the leadership phenomenon, it creates a heightened aware-ness and deepened understanding of the existential nature of authentic leadership. In this respect it is an approach that emphasises reflection and exploration of the leader's individual world view over their immedi-ate goals or performance issues.

References

1. Kernis, M. H. (2003). *Towards a conceptualization of optimal self-esteem.* Psychological Inquiry, *14*, 1–26.
2. Gardner, W. L., Avolio, B. J. & Walumbwa, F. O. (2005). *Authentic Leadership Development: Emergent themes and future directions.* In Gardener, W., Avolio, B. & Walumba, F. (Eds). *Authentic Leadership Theory and Practise: Origins, Effects and Development.* Oxford: Elsevier, 387–406.
3. Walumbwa, F. O., Avolio, B. J., Gardner, W. L., Wernsing, T. S. & Peterson, S. J. (2008) *Authentic Leadership: Development and validation of a theory based measure.* Journal of Management, *34*, 89–126.
4. Neider, L. L. & Schriesheim, C. A. (2011) *The Authentic Leadership Inventory (ALI): Development and empirical tests.* The Leadership Quarterly, *22*, 1146–1164.
5. Lawler, J. & Ashman, I. (2012). *Theorizing leadership authenticity: A Sartrean perspective.* Leadership, *8*, 327–344.
6. Hayek, M., Williams, W. A., Clayton, R. W., Novicevic. M. M. & Humphreys, J. H. (2014). *In extremis leadership of Sartrean authenticity: Examples from Xenophon's Anabasis.* Journal of Management History, *20*, 292–310.
7. Algera, P. M. & Lips-Wiersma, M. (2012). *Radical Authentic Leadership: Co-creating the conditions under which all measures of the organisation can be authentic.* Leadership Quarterly, *33*, 118–131.
8. George, B. (2007). *True North: Discover Your Authentic Leadership.* San Francisco: Jossey Bassey.
9. Peltier, B. (2001). *The Psychology of Executive Coaching.* 2nd Ed. New York: Routledge.
10. Fusco, T., O'Riordan, S. & Palmer, S. (2013). *A Group-Coaching approach to Authentic Leadership Development.* Coaching Psychology International, *6*, 9–14.
11. Fusco, T., O'Riordan, S. & Palmer, S. (2014). *A humanistic approach to Authentic Leadership Development.* Coaching Psychology International, *7*, 11–16.
12. Ford, J. & Lawler, J. (2007). *Blending existentialist and constructivist approaches in leadership studies: An exploratory account.* Leadership and Organisation Development Journal, *28*, 409–425.

3   How does it work? Part 1: Understanding the process of Authentic Leadership Group Coaching

The purpose of this chapter is twofold. The first purpose is to overview the qualitative research method used in this study and the second is to begin to introduce the findings. In this chapter, these findings will focus on the *process* of AL Group Coaching and in Chapter 5 they will focus on the *output*. To identify both of these, a research method called Grounded Theory (GT) was employed. It may be useful to summarise briefly the GT process so the reader can have a degree of understanding and confidence in it as an appropriate method of data analysis and interpretation for Authentic Leadership Development.

Grounded Theory

GT is perhaps the most respected of qualitative research methods because of its structured and systematic approach to data collection and analysis.[1] Its primary purpose is to generate theory from data through a process that codes the data into categories in an increasingly abstracted way to achieve a theoretical explanation about the phenomenon being investigated. This approach runs counter to the traditional method of empirical investigation. The usual scientific approach is to develop a hypothesis then design an experiment that tests this hypothesis through the careful control of potentially influencing extraneous factors. In contrast, GT approaches an area of investigation with no existing idea or 'theory' to explain what might be happening. Instead, it collects and interrogates data to find out what the data themselves are saying about the subject under investigation. These data, which can be collected from multiple sources such as interviews, surveys, observation, etc., is subject to various levels of coding and categorisation that eventually leads to a full conceptual understanding of the phenomena. It can be a slow and demanding process, but one that ultimately helps to develop a theoretical and explanatory model of the area of study that is robustly *grounded* in its empirical data.

GT was originally developed for sociological research,[1] but has now been widely adopted by the medical and business communities as a method of investigation and understanding of organisational behaviour. As mentioned, most existing approaches to scientific research are designed to test hypotheses that are, in some way, logically linked to an existing grand theory. GT, however, aims not to test an existing theory, but to generate a new one. In this respect, it is ideally suited to areas in which there is little or no existing theory. For that reason, it was deemed appropriate for developing a theoretical method and model of Authentic Leadership Development, for which there was no pre-existing theory.

Several GT approaches have developed over the years,[2,3] but the method used for this research was based on the original system introduced by Glaser and Strauss.[1] This approach to GT, like all versions, is based on *constant comparative analysis*, which includes several key steps such as data coding, theoretical coding, theoretical sampling and theoretical saturation. The ultimate aim of GT is not simply to describe a substantive area under investigation, but to offer a contextualised model that explains phenomena by identifying their component parts and the interrelationship between them. A thorough explanation of GT is not appropriate here, so I will just briefly summarise each of the steps so that the reader can see why and how I arrived at the group process explanation presented below and, more importantly, the leadership attributes that I later propose AL group coaching develops.

Data coding

Data are generated from various sources and constantly compared for consistent themes. The data for this research were obtained from two sources. First, there was a reflective log that each individual completed after each day of group coaching. Second, there was a recorded interview completed with each participant three months after the end of the programme. In total, there were 75 of the former and 25 of the latter. The reflective logs captured information about the process of the AL Group Coaching that we discuss here and the interview data identified the output of the ALD process that we will come on to in Chapter 5. Each log and transcribed interview was meticulously coded on a line-by-line basis for recurring themes in the data. The purpose of the coding is to sort, separate and categorise the data with codes that act to both summarise and explain that segment of data. Through this process, you also gain insight into relationships between the data. For example, based on many concrete examples in the reflective log data, an initial set of codes was identified that included *exploring motivation*, *exploring emotions* and *questioning oneself*. These were then combined and became properties of a higher level of theoretical coding, in this case a category called *self-reflection and self-exploration*.

Theoretical coding

These higher-level theoretical codes are also conceptualisations of how the various categories interact and fit together into the overall theory. To continue the example, after the codes of *exploring motivation, exploring emotions* and *questioning oneself* were abstracted into the category of *self-reflection and self-exploration*, this was then combined with two further categories of *self-learning and relearning* and *self-reappraisal and realignment* to form the category of *authentic self-development*. In terms of interconnected relationships, this overall category is classified as a *cause* category, which is predicated upon the *conditions* categories of 'group cohesion' and 'psychological safety' (discussed below) and together lead to the *consequence* category of the seven leadership attributes (discussed in Chapter 5). It is important that the theory provides explanatory links between each of the conceptual categories, otherwise it remains simply a descriptive exercise. And so, the GT process captures a timeline and causal consequence model, identifying the core relationships between conditions, causes and consequences. The conditions and causes categories are presented in this chapter, and the consequences category is presented in the next.

Theoretical sampling

This is an important part of the constant comparison method and means you actively sample theoretically relevant data. At first, this is achieved simply by the creation of ALD coaching groups that are purposively populated by suitable individuals at appropriate levels of leadership. Then after data capture and analysis has commenced, it advances with a continual back-and-forth cross-referencing of the data, using both within-group comparison and between-group comparison. Something that makes GT distinct from the hypothesis-testing scientific approach is that you collect and analyse data as the research progresses and, as theoretical codes begin to emerge, you test and investigate that data for further examples and properties. In this research, this process included reconvening some of the groups to examine the categories that had begun to emerge. This allowed collection of further evidence of their properties that, in turn, makes the categories more theoretically dense and moves them towards *theoretical saturation*.

Theoretical saturation

The constant comparative method, comparing *within*-group data and *between*-group data, interview to interview and log to log, enabled the GT process eventually to reach theoretical saturation; that is, no new codes, properties, categories or relationships emerged and all new data simply occupied existing categories. This eventually induces a theory integrated at various conceptual levels; in this model, conditional, causal and consequential. Ultimately, the objective of theory building is to identify something that can offer understanding and explanation; in practical terms, this means you know what's happening and why.

For AL Group Coaching, this level of understanding and explanation offers two benefits. First, it helps illuminate what is going on throughout the process; and second, it identifies the exact benefits of the process. In this respect, it helps answer our second and third questions: *how* does AL Group Coaching work and *what* does 'work' actually mean? In the section to follow, I shall concentrate on the first of these two questions and explain how AL Group Coaching actually works.

Group conditions

In each of the groups that made up this research, every member was asked to complete a reflective log after every session. These logs were then analysed and coded according to the GT protocol to gain a thorough understanding of what was happening within the group process as it developed. From this analysis, two group conditions and three group processes were identified. The two group conditions or 'building blocks' identified were: *group cohesion* and *psychological safety* (See Figure 3.1).

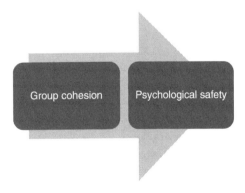

Figure 3.1 Group conditions

Group cohesion

It is satisfying to see how purposive sampling helps groups cohere. This isn't just critical for research purposes, but also for practical and real-world application as well. How many of us have worked in groups that are made up of a collection of talented individuals who, for whatever reason, simply cannot work effectively together? In the time-limited AL coaching group, group cohesion is identified as a crucial factor that seems to be the bedrock upon which all further individual and group work takes place. So, despite what might seem an inherent bias in purposive participant selection, it actually contributes to group efficiency[4] by helping to create groups that cohere quickly and start achieving tangible results from day 1. Composite quotes from participants may give the reader a sense of what this actually feels like to group members:

> *Great to meet, gain understanding of and build a level of trust and achieve a degree of camaraderie within the group. The easy-going format generated good team spirit from the outset and the highly participative sessions worked well and enabled people to "bed in" to the event. The group sessions are incredibly supportive, enlightening and very encouraging. This, in itself, is one of the tremendous features of the programme.*

Psychological safety

Importantly, this sense of group cohesion facilitates the development of the next building block of the whole process, which is psychological safety. If cohesion is the group's bedrock, then psychological safety is the individuals'. Psychological safety provides the individual with a sufficient level of comfort and confidence that enables them to tolerate a degree of vulnerability in discussing themselves in the group in a way that is necessary for effective ALD to occur. Again, from a small selection of quotes, the reader may get a sense of what this actually looks and feels like to participants:

> *I think the group itself gelled very well and therefore it gives a comfortable environment to be honest in and explore. I felt safe in divulging my story. I soon realised we were all in the same boat and quickly felt comfortable and easily able to be open. I felt that the participants worked well together and we soon all felt happy sharing our thoughts and views.*

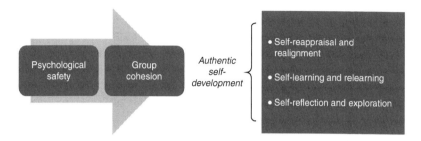

Figure 3.2 AL Group Coaching process

Once these conditions are firmly established, the group work can begin in earnest. Here, the research identified a distinct three-part hierarchical process undertaken by participants that is very similar to existing self-system processes already identified by other researchers that include at their centre attention, cognition and regulation.[5] Here, the GT data clearly identified *self-reflection and exploration, self-learning and relearning* and *self-reappraisal and realignment* (Figure 3.2).

Self-reflection and self-exploration

When the conditions of group cohesion and psychological safety have been successfully established, they facilitate individual introspection and enable the individual to undertake the deep reflective thinking necessary for genuine Authentic Leadership Development. Once again this is illustrated by participant quotes:

> *I find myself asking the question, "Who am I?" Drawing upon my new-found self-awareness and looking inwards and searching for values, meaning and self-identity. I had a strong but very positive sense of being in uncharted territory. I look forward very much to the next session as a way of thinking deeper about some of my past professional and personal experiences.*

Self-learning and relearning

Following reflection and exploration come varying degrees of increased self-insight and learning. This can take many forms including intrapersonal learning, both cognitive and emotional, and interpersonal learning, both behavioural and relational. Some of these insights appear genuinely new to individuals and some appear as if they are being relearnt, having been once forgotten or otherwise put from everyday conscious thought. Again, personal quotes give us an insight into this learning:

> *After the first day, I had a long think about myself as a person and not just a manager. It did make me realise that how I am as a manager is not mirrored in how I am as a person. This has now changed and it's very enlightening to realise how comfortable your own authentic style can be, feels a bit like relearning a language you once knew. It gave me a clear realisation that I'd changed or been trying to fit into a style that wasn't really me.*

Self-reappraisal and realignment

The final part of this process – one that seems predicated upon the previous two – is an internal shift that seems to represent a form of 'self-recalibration'. Initially, this takes place internally as an adjustment to how individuals see the world and themselves within it, but is then invariably followed by external and overt changes. These cover a broad spectrum of behavioural and relational changes, but they represent a natural change based upon the reflection and learning that has taken place prior to this stage. So, what individuals appear to achieve is significant and enduring psychological, emotional and behavioural development that remains long after the group intervention has concluded.

> *Being part of this group is proving to be very inspiring and motivating. It's influencing the way I approach not just leadership, but many aspects of my life. The process of investigating my own values, personality traits and temperament, and then directly linking these to a personal reference for authentic behaviour, has had a deeply motivating influence on me. It encourages you to focus on your own authenticity and gives you courage and confidence to think and do things in your own way. It's having a profound and constant effect on my everyday thoughts and approach to life.*

Hopefully, the analysis above helps to capture and illustrate what the process of AL Group Coaching entails from both a theoretical and a participant perspective. It is also hoped that, through briefly outlining the process of GT, the reader has a reasonable understanding of and confidence in the conceptual underpinning of this new approach to Authentic Leadership Development.

References

1. Glaser, B. G. & Strauss, A. L. (1967). *The Discovery of Grounded Theory: Strategies for Qualitative Research.* New York: Aldine.
2. Charmaz, K. (2014). *Constructing Grounded Theory.* London: Sage.
3. Corbin, J. M. & Strauss, A. (1990). *Grounded theory research: Procedures, canons, and evaluative criteria.* Qualitative Sociology, *13*, 3–21.
4. Tongco, M. D. C. (2007). *Purposive sampling as a tool for informant selection.* Ethnobotany Research & Applications, *5*, 147–158.
5. Mischel, W. & Morf, C. C. (2003). *The self as a psycho-social dynamic processing system: A meta-perspective on a century of the self in psychology.* In Leary, M. R. & Tangney, J.P. (Eds). *Handbook of Self and Identity*, New York: Guilford Press, 23, 15–43.

4   How does it work? Part 2: The Authentic Leader's self-concept

Authentic Leadership's core maxims to 'know thyself' and 'to thine own self be true' have as their focal point the issue of self. If this self is to be both known and owned as an Authentic Leader, then it should sit at the centre of any discussion of Authentic Leadership Development.

The self has many definitions and is an idea long discussed historically by social philosophers and, more recently, clinical, developmental and cognitive psychologists. Despite this broad church, however, there seems to be an emerging consensus around the idea that the self is a dynamic system that includes both an interpersonal and an intrapersonal element.[1] It is now believed to be an organised system made up of both an internal cognitive–emotional system and an external socially constructed system. Both aspects of this self-system operate and interact at multiple levels interchangeably and concurrently and reflect how people think about themselves, both in terms of description and evaluation. For example, I may have a concept of myself that I describe in terms of intelligence, personality, motivations, etc., but I will also judge these aspects, too. And as I will probably describe these aspects of my self in comparison to others, so too will I almost inevitably judge them in comparison to others as well. There is also mounting evidence that the self-system has both a *core self-concept* – one that is coherent and consistent across time – and a more readily accessible and malleable *working self-concept*, which is more subject to and influenced by ongoing social interaction and activation.

The Self-Concept Clarity Scale

Self-concept clarity is the degree to which an individual's self-concept is consistent and stable across time. It was considered important to establish whether AL Group Coaching has the power to increase this clarity in a leader. To this end, the Self-Concept Clarity Scale (SCCS)[2] was

Table 4.1 SCCS *t*-test scores

Self-concept clarity	Mean difference	Standard deviation	*t*	*df*	Significance (*two-tailed*)
SCCS scores	8.32	8.27	−5.03	24	0.001

used, which is a 12-item, 5-point scale that has strong validity and reliability in terms of both temporal stability and internal consistency. The SCCS assessment questionnaire was completed by each leader at the beginning of day 1 and at the end of day 3, three months later.

The SCCS scores showed high statistical significance at $t = 5.03$, $p<0.001$. The p-value shows that the probability of the leader's score difference being produced by chance is less than 1 in 1000. Against the usual cut-off point of $p<0.05$ or 5 per cent, this score is highly significant. The Cohen effect size was again calculated and showed a large effect size of $d = 1.01$, indicating these participants were likely to score higher than 84 per cent of a control group. These results allow us to conclude that AL Group Coaching does significantly increase a leader's self-concept clarity, indicating that they are able to access and modify their self-concept during the group coaching process – certainly their working self-concept and very possibly their core self-concept as well, as discussed below.

One reason for this effectiveness in working at the level of the self may well be that the group coaching also operates interchangeably and concurrently at the multiple levels that the self-system does. The group coaching structure allows it to target both internally constructed aspects of the self-system along with the socially constructed aspects of the system (i.e. how I think about me, how I think others think about me and what I actually feel about each of those). It achieves this through the intrapersonal focus the leader has while working *in* the group and the interpersonal focus they have working *with* the group. It appears that the group process enables individuals to reach their more readily accessible *working self-concept* through the group process and to explore and experiment with the various self-conceptions held within it. It may also be possible through this process for change to occur at the underlying core self-concept level, as suggested in one individual's report below.

"It was the exorcism of my ghost!"

Lewis was the managing director of a highly technical manufacturing company with a global reach. He'd had a glowing career that had taken him to the top and yet he remained plagued by imposter syndrome. *Imposter syndrome is characterised by a leader's persistent belief that they aren't up to the job and those who think they are must be foolish. They feel that they got where they are by fluke and that any day they will be found out for the fake that they are. It can be a considerable psychic burden to carry, which Lewis had felt throughout his entire leadership career since rising from the ranks of engineer. To look at him you would say he identified very strongly with his leadership persona. Yet beneath it all, it was clear that his leadership self-concept was shaky. Through the group process, Lewis was able to reappraise and recalibrate this self-concept, which allowed him to return to work just in time to take up an even greater global role with new-found certainty in himself and his leadership.*

"*The experience was a really deep dive into who I am – my strengths, my weaknesses and almost an exorcism of the ghost that I think I've had for a while... the demon that's classically known as the imposter syndrome. The breakthrough for me was to finally believe that if everyone else thinks you're good enough... then you're good enough. So, leave the imposter here at the end of the last day and go back and have the confidence to just get stuck in... which was fantastic for me! The transition to my new role is really heavy but I find myself falling back on this to help me deal with the workload and responsibilities. I'm under considerable pressure in my new role but I do fall back upon this as a protection device to keep my head above water. Banishing the imposter yields an improvement in my performance because I'm less stressed and therefore undertaking my tasks more efficiently. If I'm feeling I'm the right man in the right job and not having lingering doubts about when they'll discover me, then there must be a benefit in my performance in terms of efficiency and effectiveness because I'm not dwelling on things and not having doubts but thinking this is what we need to do and then getting on and doing it! Then move on to the next challenge. This has helped with the engagement of my new group of global CEOs and going out to the subsidiaries and engaging with the management teams as the new boss and dealing with the new parent company stakeholders. So upstream and downstream my performance has improved in terms of efficiency and effectiveness which must then also yield a business benefit of how I'm performing in my new Ops role. There has always been an actor aspect of me. In the past, I'd always imagine the part that's expected of me and act it – but now there's less acting and more authenticity.*"

It is perhaps worthy of note that this leader had already had several individual coaching sessions previously, but it took joining an ALD group to create the seismic shift required to alter both his working and core self-concepts. This individual was followed-up with a year later and still these changes in self-concept remained.

Possible selves

The self-concept has within it a wide variety of different individual self-conceptions: the good, the bad and the ugly ones, the ought-to and should-do ones, even the hoped-for and ideal ones.[3] At any one moment, the working self-concept represents one of many possible constellations that are activated by a particular social context and situation. The working self-concept is malleable and temporary, as what it is experiencing at any given moment will depend on what the social environment evokes (Figure 4.1). The core self-concept, on the other hand, appears relatively stable and the variety of sub self-conceptions held within it remain consistent. The smaller variety of core self-conceptions remain consistent overall, although some will be more significant and central and others more peripheral. To illustrate this point, consider how you are when you are talking to your staff, then your own boss, then your children, your partner, your best friend or your siblings. Each situation will trigger and elicit a different working self-concept. They are all still you, but each different social encounter evokes a different working version of your self-concept, making it more accessible and dominant by bringing it into working memory. New self-conceptions can be added and others can become more or less active over time, but overall they give a certain sense of integration, structure and coherence to our core self-concept. This also suggests that there is no single, unifying, monolithic self that represents an individual in their entirety. The self-concept is diverse, complex and multifaceted. Consider a large jewel with its many sides. Each side reflects and refracts light in different ways as the stone moves and reacts to the light in its environment. The many and different sides of your self are also illuminated and brought to life depending on the prevailing conditions and requirements of your environment.

Our core self-concept reaches far back in time and through its evolution has developed a whole subset of these sub and working self-concepts. In addition to this host of existing *actual* self-concepts, there is also a myriad of *possible* new self-concepts that represent development, growth and change.[3] The idea of the *possible self* is important to Authentic Leadership Development because it can represent a new stage on an individual's developmental journey. Importantly, it is also a conceptual link between our past, present and future and, as such, gives meaning, organisation and direction towards that future. When we attempt to move towards a possible self, this puts into operation tangible mediators such as motivations, behaviours and goals. These in turn help us approach a desired possible self or even move away from an undesired one. Consider an individual who sees a possible self as a particularly qualified professional one day. They then translate that long-term vision of a possible self into concrete behaviours and goals in the short and mid-term, such as embarking on a course of studies rather than travelling the world or writing a novel. The desired possible self therefore provides evaluation criteria against which one can calibrate and recalibrate existing behaviours and goals. In this context, though, goals aren't just related to specific tasks or performance, but are also related to the more global goals regarding what a person wants to achieve or become longer term. So, in the pursuit of authenticity, both distal and proximal goals should cohere, meaning goals and behaviours are concordant and self-determined.[4] Next, we look more closely at the working self-concept and consider how this can also be given structure and coherence towards a future possible self through appropriately congruent goals and behaviours.

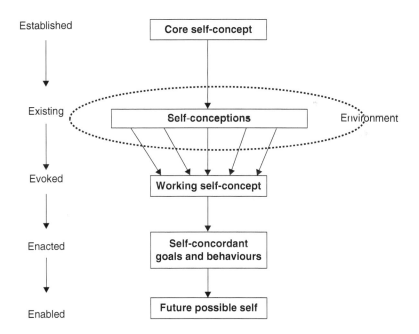

Figure 4.1 Relationship between core/working self-concepts and the possible self

Self-concordant goals

In terms of goal systems, it can be said that the self is coherent and integrated when goal systems cohere both horizontally and vertically and when they are freely chosen and intrinsically satisfying.[5] Vertical coherence is a hierarchical structure where the 'lower goals' are consistent with and feed into the 'higher goal' as in the pursuit of a desired future possible self. In organisational terms, it would be the same as aligning lower-level tasks and objectives with mid-level strategy, which, in turn, helps to achieve the company's high-level vision or mission. In addition to the low–high connection, there also needs to be horizontal connections at the same levels within the hierarchy, so that the achievement of one goal at this level contributes to the success of another. Again, in organisational terms, the goals of sales, marketing, product R&D and manufacturing should all be aligned. The achievement of goals in one division is instrumental for success in the others, whereas failure in one undermines the overall organisational goal structure. On an individual level, if I want to realise a country promotion, I might first have to take an overseas assignment to achieve the experience missing from my CV. So, moving to Singapore for three years may be highly congruent with my ambition of a UK directorship. Integration in either a personal or professional domain ideally sees both vertical and horizontal goals systemically connected and coherent. Consider the leader vignette below that shows how an individual changed his goals and his role to be more aligned with who and what he believed he was as a leader – a thought leader, not a staff leader.

> ***"I'm a good leader… but in a different way."***
> *Martin is a health service IT director. He is an innovative thinker with a passion for how IT can be integrated to make life easier for his organisational users and the public at large. Unfortunately, as is often the case, the best technician got the job of heading up the team of technicians. Martin persevered, but his inability to deal with the 'nuts and bolts' of senior management was taking its toll on him, his team and his department. And importantly, it was impacting his own self-concept as an effective leader, which he truly believed he was, but, as it turned out, just in a different way.*
> *"I hadn't realised how unhappy I'd been for such a long time. But the group work has led me to thinking – this is the sort of person I am, and I'm really good at it. And history tells me I'm really good at it. I've learnt so much about myself and that I am a good leader and capable of doing great things. I'm just not a general manager and I was*

asked to be a general manager and it was killing me! I couldn't even make decisions on whether we should hire or fire someone. I do believe I'm a good leader but not a good general manager… I'm different. It's made me think differently. I've gone from a really frustrating, almost agonising place to a position of absolute clarity. The group pulled out of me things I really didn't appreciate about myself, some of the ways I'm driven, my wiring and my unique way of looking at things and helped me understand myself more. It's made me feel much more at ease with who and what I am. As a result, I'm no longer heading up Tech Solutions but have taken up a different Strategic Tech role so I can get involved in setting the strategy and implementing the plan and dealing with the big decisions around that."

However, in terms of personal and leadership authenticity, a goal system doesn't just need coherence – it also needs to be self-determined and self-congruent; that is, congruent with the needs of the self-concept and the related behaviours that will help movement towards an envisioned possible self. Such self-concordant goals are more intrinsically motivating and genuinely satisfying and, because they have an internal locus of causality and control, they do not need the external regulation that often comes with extrinsically motivated goals and behaviour. Consequently, ideas of congruence, coherence and concordance are all implicated in positive psychological adjustment.[5] Though this idea has already been introduced by various theorists over the years with humanistic, psychodynamic and cognitive theories of development, evidence from this research supports the theory that, given the right conditions, a healthy individual's tendency is indeed towards growth and integration – what we might term a *cohesive expansion* of the self.

There are of course many other facets pertinent to the self-system, such as emotion, motivation, etc., but it is the three interconnected processes of attention, cognition and regulation that are seen as being fundamental to the construction of the self-concept. It is apparent ALD Group Coaching participants go through this internal, three-part, attention–cognition–regulation process, as was identified through the GT analysis that resulted in the causal categories of self-awareness and exploration, self-learning and relearning and self-appraisal and realignment. Consider the two leader vignettes below that demonstrate these in action.

"Looking back made me move forward."

Katherine was a director in the finance sector. She had suffered a considerable setback in her career when a role in which she was deputising was taken from her and reassigned elsewhere. This was a huge blow that had badly shaken her confidence and was continuing to have repercussions in her new role and with her new team. For Katherine, the group process enabled her to fully understand how this aspect of her current working self-concept was plaguing her with a vicious circle of negative thinking and self-handicapping behaviour. Going through the group coaching enabled her to return to work brimming with a restored self-confidence that naturally accompanied the change in her working self-concept.

"What was really powerful about the lifeline exercise was sharing it with the group. Standing in front of everybody and going through and articulating it was a profoundly enlightening exercise. Because whilst you know what's affected you, when you have to try and articulate the points in your life that were high and low and why does then make you look at what it's done to you as a person. I knew I'd always felt a bit lacking in confidence when my role changed, but I think it helped me realise what it had done and how it had affected me, and how I was now responsible for my own future destiny. People had been saying that to me for ages and my previous boss had said only I can let this go. But it was only really talking in the group environment that I really fully understood that no one else was going to take this away from me. No one can change it… only me. That changed my whole view and I came back to work in a much more positive way. It was a really powerful experience. I've had more than one person comment that they could see a difference in me after day 1 because it made me realise how I'm the one who owns my future destiny. Rather than feel the situation was one that was done to me and feeling a bit wounded about it and that it was everyone else's fault and letting that run on and on – the difference was I was suddenly able to think… c'mon, only you can actually do anything about this, it's never going to get wiped away so you can either get on with it and learn from it or just carry on… and I didn't want to carry on so I thought, 'Well, alright then, get a grip girl.' It made me realise that I could carry on listening to that and continue carrying that in my head, but really that's not what I wanted… I wanted to feel like I feel now. Looking back made me move forward… it made me move forward because I wanted to move forward! It let me get back to the person I was… and I'm back to feeling how I felt years ago. I feel completely different and it was the past that was holding me back. My previous boss had often said, 'You have to let it go because if you don't it will hang round your neck.' It's no good just being told that, but when you eventually say it out loud you actually think… yes, that is right! I now recognise

that nobody else can get me to that end point. What all this did from my perspective was to make me think about – what it was in the past that was holding me back, where I get stuck in the present and in the future what my goals were. So that journey has made me think that if that's what's affecting me, then surely I have to think about that for my team. Opening my eyes as to what I needed to operate and be most effective has made me realise that I want to be empowered so therefore with my team I should do exactly the same. So, it's helped me pass on that clarity. In one of the sessions I began wondering, 'Where do I get stuck that doesn't allow me to do my job properly?' So, I thought of the horizon, the long grass and the weeds and this was a real eye-opener for me because everything in the weeds was where I was really focussing, that's where I was stuck all the time – bits of detail, bits of stuff, bits of this and that coming through the door. It was a wholesale need to rethink. I'm in a completely different place. I feel I'm in a place where I know what's happening, I know where I'm going. It's been the thing that's unlocked everything else I've done since and I don't think I'd be where I am if I hadn't have done it."

"I never understood what 'lose the emotion' meant."

Colette is a service manager within a charity organisation and found it easy to be passionate and impassioned by the work she did. The organisation provides a very human service and Colette has a deep commitment to its cause. The downside of this is that sometimes the amount of energy she expends in her role depletes her stores and leaves her exhausted. She also noticed that sometimes the level of emotion clouds issues with both her staff and the people they serve. She is an individual who is committed to personal and professional development, but says the perennial advice she gets of 'losing the emotion' has always remained an elusive piece of the jigsaw for her. Once again, the group format enabled her to access this aspect of her working self-concept, which in turn allowed her to fundamentally change it, practically overnight.

"People have said to me in the past, 'Lose the emotion.' I recognise in many situations, particularly with managing staff and the passion around what we do and in terms of the standards and outcomes I expect, this emotion has really served me well, and so I just didn't have clarity or couldn't ever understand in a concrete way what that actually meant – 'Lose the emotion.' It used to really get on my nerves and I just didn't understand it. So, the greatest learning for me is that now I absolutely do understand that in concrete terms.

It's about recognising that balance and that 'yes' in many ways the emotion serves me, but actually there are occasions when it absolutely doesn't and I need to behave and respond to people in a different way. I've learnt it's about moving from a place of emotional response to pausing and thinking, 'How do I need to respond to this?' It's a daily practice for me now, hitting the pause button and thinking, 'How do I actually want to respond to this, what's going to serve me here?' A downside to responding to everything in an emotional way is that it has a cost, energy-wise. I have much more of an awareness now of choosing different ways of responding to situations that arise in the workplace. It's a consciousness that I didn't have before. It's phenomenal learning for me because I'd been told this over and over again and I just didn't get it, but it's now somehow crystallised and I now understand what it means on a daily basis. That wouldn't have happened if it hadn't been for the group. It's one thing to receive info on your own, but to actually discuss it in depth with the group is really something else and extremely beneficial. Behaviour change has been very concrete for me because how I respond to things has changed enormously. Things in the past that I would have dispelled all sorts of emotional energy on just don't now affect me in the same way. I used to get triggered by all the craziness around me but now... it's extraordinary really... it's happened over and over and over again since we finished, but now I can somehow just pause, take a breath and choose how I'm going to respond. Just sticking to the facts now and not going to a place of emotion has served me so well, it's amazing, and I'm not losing energy like I did, which is fantastic. It's so freeing in a way because I don't invest the same amount of energy somehow. I feel much calmer. There are sometimes when it's useful and I'll continue to do that but now I have clarity – I have a choice! It's been a revelation for me, whereas before it was a conundrum... for years and years. I think I was doing a phenomenal job before but with this it has taken it to a completely different level. I've realised to prove myself I don't have to exhaust myself!"

Both of these vignettes are more clear examples of how intelligent and motivated people don't need to be shown how or what to change. They sometimes just need greater clarity and understanding of how they shape their self-concepts. When they achieve this self-awareness and insight, then desired change can and usually does follow, easily and naturally. It is what is known as 'paradoxical change' – the natural change that readily occurs when the cohesive expansion referred to earlier takes place, when you are allowed to become more of what you are, rather than forced to become more of what you're not.

We have discussed what happens intrapersonally with participants situated inside the group, so the next questions to be addressed are: what happens at the interpersonal level within the group and what has the power to trigger these sorts of personal changes within its members? In the section below, we shall explore these questions and look at how the social forces within the group help participants access and alter their working and core self-concepts.

The social self within the group

There is a long tradition of research into the self that acknowledges the importance of social interaction in the construction and modification of the self-concept.[6,7,8] Many researchers share the idea that the self is publicly constructed and exists not exclusively, but primarily in relation to others.[9,10] Such theorists have developed ideas that provide insight into the social functioning of the coaching group, in particular the interpersonal aspect of the process. For example, the theory of symbolic interactionism[5] argues that it is at the level of human interaction and interpersonal relationships that the self actually arises; that the self is fluid, not fixed, and is a project that the individual actively builds and develops throughout his or her life in the social and interpersonal context in which they are embedded. Along similar lines, the concept of the *reflected self*[7] suggests that the self develops in the social environment and the whole concept of the self cannot be separated from social influences, actually being built by assimilating the reflected appraisals of others. The idea of *reflected appraisal*[9] suggests that people develop their self-concepts on the basis of the perceived attitudes of others towards them and through a process of social comparison we evaluate ourselves by comparing ourselves with other people, groups and social categories. All of these theories share the idea that the self-concept is a fundamentally social phenomenon, constructed and modified through ongoing social interaction. The idea that the self is not fixed, but is actively constructed and reconstructed within a social context, can help explain why the AL coaching group proves such a fertile environment for personal growth and change. Consider another vignette below to hear these ideas in action and how they can act as a catalyst for the attention–cognition–regulation processes discussed earlier that help shape the working self-concept. You will hear how the reflected appraisals from other group members practically stopped this leader dead in their tracks, acting as the clarion call for the considerable self-reflection and reassessment that followed.

"*I never thought I'd be an issue for anyone in the workplace.*"

Laura is an HR director in the public sector and a bold and somewhat maverick character. She has gained significant 'life' experience outside her organisational life, which has given her an independence and forthrightness in thought and spirit that some of her colleagues can find somewhat challenging. Laura had various personal support mechanisms in place, including both individual counselling and coaching, yet the group environment proved crucial for her to fully appreciate the impact her behaviour could have on her relationships at work.

"I remember when I looked at my lifeline and I just stood there and went 'Wow!' I looked at it and thought that's just... it's just... well, it was quite shocking. It shocked me as I've never seen it like that before. I just tend to do each bit and think, 'That's that bit done,' and move on. I've never seen it joined up as one great big thing before. The enormity of everything that has happened just hit me. And the comment that stuck with me for ages was when another person in the group asked me, 'Do you choose to live your life in chaos?' I've just never viewed my life like that. It made me think about the first impression I give people – it gave me a perception of how people may see me at work that I'd never really thought of before. The pace at which I work is quite frenetic so I don't really notice how other people are with me or how they might perceive me. I found one particular group member quite difficult and challenging at times and it did make me think about how someone like him would perceive me and cope with me in the workplace. I remember he said to me one day, 'How do people cope with you in the workplace?' and I've never thought about that. I don't think I'm that challenging in the workplace. I've never looked back and thought someone might find that really hard to deal with, I've never thought of it like that. Now if I'm going into a meeting to meet new people I'm conscious of that and I will actively try and be on my best behaviour now. What it did make me realise is that I never thought I would be an issue for anyone in the workplace. I'm just the way I am and I've never considered that people might find that difficult. My team would probably tell you I'm more communicative with them now and that I spend more time with them. I try to let them know more what's going on and I've got more open with them about what I'm like and what I need from them. They've all said that I'm better at communicating with them now and that I now understand what it is they need from me better because now I can see that very few of them

*have got the characteristics that I've got. I thought I was quite good at
communicating with them before but I can now see that either I wasn't
giving them the info they wanted or in the way that they needed. They
now say that we work together better as a team, we spend more time
together and they say it feels more cohesive."*

However, not all social interaction is equally important in the development of the self-concept. It is the *primary* interactions with *significant others* that are considered the most influential.[6] It was symbolic
interactionism that first introduced the term *significant other*, proposing
that we develop and negotiate our sense of self through internal and
external dialogue with these significant others in our social sphere. In
Sources of the Self, Taylor[11] also describes how identity depends on such
internalised *dialogical relations* with these significant others, even when
they disappear from our lives. ALD group members have described
how they tend to carry the group around with them in their heads and
continue to converse with them between meetings. In this respect, the
group can also take the form of what Mead[6] describes as a *generalised
other*. He believed an inner conversation goes on between this generalised other and the individual and that this significant reference group
then becomes an integral part of a person's thinking and, in this way,
contributes to their sense of self. Mirroring these theories, it would seem
that each of the ALD group members becomes a *significant other* to
each other member and that the coaching group as a whole becomes a
significant *generalised other* to its members. In this way, each member
and the group as a whole join the constellation of already existing *significant others* capable of influencing each member's self-appraisal and
self-concept as they continue to have internal dialogical relationships
with them.

It is worth commenting, however, that there is a balance between a
person's autonomy and the influence of others – and that the self that
depends exclusively on the appraisal of others is probably a compara-
tively weak and unstable self. So, this raises the question, along with the
significant other and the *generalised other*, which appraisals are given
more importance over others? Gergen[12] investigated this question and
looked at the specific factors that make some people's appraisal more
likely to influence an individual's self-evaluation than others. In looking at these factors, I shall map them here onto a typical AL coaching
group. Gergen first asserts that the other person has to be seen as *cred-
ible*. This is invariably the case, as ALD group members are purposively
selected as motivated, intelligent and successful professionals in their
respective fields. Second, they have to be experienced by the individual

as *personable* rather than impersonal. Again, this is most often the case in the ALD group, as inclusion criteria to the group require the ability to relate constructively to others, even when challenging or being challenged. Third, there are *subsequent confirming appraisals* by others. This again is often witnessed, as it is common to see similarity in the reflected appraisals of the group members, particularly if they are reflecting back to an individual an observation of a blind spot that is apparent to the group but obscured from the individual's own self-view. A final important factor that makes an appraisal more likely to affect an individual's self-concept is if it comes from a member of a relevant group, considered a *significant generalised other* by that individual. As already mentioned, I have found that, almost without exception, the Authentic Leadership group does indeed assume such a position for each of its members.

I believe these theories offer some illuminating insight into some of the parallel processes operating within the unique format of the Authentic Leadership coaching group and why this group environment seems so potent at affecting change, development and growth. There is a myriad of social dynamics at play at any one time, including social comparison choices, reflected appraisals and the evaluation or anticipated evaluation of others that these bring. But we should remember that, while these all still have relevance, only we know of the family of alternative self-conceptions we live with. Only we can securely place ourselves within our past, our present and our hoped-for future. Only we really know of how our present self sits in comparison to our past selves and how that compares to the potential possible self we may aspire one day to become. Only we ultimately know who and what our authentic self really is.

References

1. Mischel, W. & Morf, C. C. (2003). *The self as a psycho-social dynamic processing system: A meta-perspective on a century of the self in psychology.* In Leary, M.R. & Tangney, J.P. (Eds). *Handbook of Self and Identity.* New York: Guilford Press, 23 15–43.
2. Campbell, J. D., Trapnell, P. D., Heine, S. J., Katz, I. M., Lavalle, L. F. & Lehman, D. R. (1996) *Self-concept clarity: Measurement, personality correlates and cultural boundaries.* Journal of Personality and Social Psychology, *70*, 141–156.
3. Markus, H. & Nurius, P. (1986). *Possible selves.* American Psychologist, *41*, 954–969.
4. Deci, E. L. & Ryan, R. M. (2010). *Self-Determination.* Toronto, Canada: John Wiley & Sons, Inc.

5. Sheldon, K. M. & Kasser, T. (1995). *Coherence and congruence: Two aspects of personality integration*. Journal of Personality and Social Psychology, 68, 531–543.

6. Mead, G. H. (1934). *Mind, Self and Society: From the Standpoint of a Social Behaviourist*. Chicago: University of Chicago Press.

7. James, W. (1890). *The Principles of Psychology*. Cambridge: Harvard University Press.

8. Cooley, C. H. (1902). *Human Nature and the Social Order*. New York: Scribner's.

9. Rosenberg, M. (1979). *Conceiving the Self*. New York: Basic Books.

10. Baumeister, R. F. (1982). *A self-presentational view of social phenomena*. Psychological Bulletin, 91, 3–26.

11. Taylor, C. (1989). *Sources of the self: The Making of the Modern Identity*. Cambridge: Harvard University Press.

12. Gergen, K. J. (1971). *The Concept of Self*. New York: Holt.

5 What does 'work' actually mean? The leadership benefits of Authentic Leadership Development

John Wanamaker (1838–1922) is often talked of as one of the first pioneers of marketing. He was a hugely successful American merchant who opened the country's first and most successful department store that grew into a chain of over a dozen stores and eventually led the way to the famous Macy's brand. One of his most famous quotes goes along the lines of "I know half of the money I spend on advertising is wasted, the trouble is I just don't know which half." This sentence I believe could also be applied to most corporate learning and development simply because it is so complex to isolate the direct correlation between the L&D that occurs in the classroom and overall organisational performance. There are simply too many influencing variables between cause and effect, particularly in the increasingly volatile and complex modern business landscape. This challenge also applies to non-profit organisations, non-governmental organisations (NGOs) and charities, as all still face the logistical and financial pressures that force them to compete and deliver in their respective fields. I think the questions addressed in this book regarding the efficacy of Authentic Leadership Development are fundamental and should be asked of any leadership programme – it makes simple business and common sense.

The story is no different for Authentic Leadership Development. In fact, the situation is probably worse. Due to the potentially ethereal perception of the term 'Authentic Leadership', some people are understandably suspicious or cynical about the concept and its potential business benefits. I personally consider this perception fair and reasonable, indeed inevitable, and for that exact reason conducted this research. So as to answer such concerns in as scientifically robust a way as possible and through the iterative evaluation of the programme development, achieve evidence-based answers to all of the three questions regarding

AL Group Coaching's efficacy; does it work, how does it work and what does 'work' actually mean?

To answer question 2 and understand how AL Group Coaching works, I left behind the quantitative evaluation tools and moved to Grounded Theory, and the same is the case for question 3, asking what the actual *output* of AL Group Coaching is. The GT process identified seven of what I have termed 'Authentic Leadership attributes'. I am conscious that this could be seen as another example of an authentic leadership competency framework; however, it isn't. These aren't skills or traits per se – they are more akin to qualities, qualities that increase a leader's sense of authenticity in their leadership role but also lead to demonstrable behaviour change and performance improvement. The crucial difference is that I am proposing these seven attributes are proven qualities that leaders develop having gone through the AL Group Coaching, as opposed to a list of predetermined learning objectives that participants are expected to achieve if they are to become authentic leaders (discussed in Chapter 7). Not everyone develops all of them, indeed not everyone needs to. But the research demonstrates that everyone who goes through the programme develops a unique combination of the seven, which they in turn use in their own unique, specific way according to their own needs and priorities. To reiterate, I am not proposing that these seven qualities form a model of Authentic Leadership – I am stating that if you were to go through the group coaching approach to ALD discussed here, these are the attributes that you would see degrees of development in.

Output data were analysed from transcribed participant interviews conducted three months after their respective groups had finished. The purpose of this was to leave a sufficient gap between their last ALD group day and the follow-up interview to allow for the natural atrophy that invariably follows many leadership development events. Astonishingly, longitudinal interviews conducted with some participants revealed that changes even remained in place up to three years later, further evidence of the paradoxical change referred to earlier. The interviews were designed to gather data at two typical levels of leadership development evaluation, discussed in depth in Chapter 7; what did the leader learn, how did they apply and implement that learning and how did that improve their performance? The rationale for this form of evaluation is that it focuses the leader on linking learning to actual behaviour change and performance improvement. Systematic interrogation of the data through the GT process identified seven key outcomes that emerged from the group coaching along with four overarching concepts that encapsulate them and give us our overall evidence-based model of Authentic Leadership Development.

Output of AL Group Coaching

The seven core categories of cognitive, behavioural, emotional and motivational change that were identified are defined and explained below.

Self-understanding and self-management

This is self-awareness that fosters greater self-control and mastery. It is an attribute that represents an increase in cognitive, emotional and motivational awareness. It also includes an increase in the effective self-regulation in each of these domains that such understanding can engender; for example, gaining greater insight into established behaviour patterns and the development of potential alternatives. Composite interview data are presented below to give a sense of what insights this raised self-awareness achieves and the self-regulation that it promotes.

> *I do now stop myself and give myself more time to think. Normally my attitude has been quite cavalier about things, say a disciplinary, if it feels right then let's get rid of them. But since this programme, I've actually been giving myself time to sleep on things first and this has*

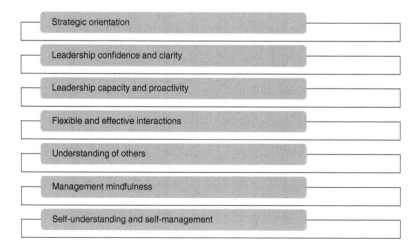

Strategic orientation

Leadership confidence and clarity

Leadership capacity and proactivity

Flexible and effective interactions

Understanding of others

Management mindfulness

Self-understanding and self-management

Figure 5.1 Seven attributes developed in Authentic Leadership Group Coaching

often led to a completely different view on things in the morning, not just on disciplinaries but on some pretty major decisions, nothing's going to change in the course of 24 hours!

Management mindfulness

This relates to a considered and deliberate execution of management duties. It is a more thoughtful approach to the functional tasks of management. One example might be thinking more carefully about a task of delegation – not just what to delegate, but to *who* and *why* and *how*? Individuals describe this attribute in this way:

> *I've created an atmosphere and an environment where I'm able to do much better quality thinking and delivery of that part of my job. So, the fundamental quality of thought process and output is just better. I feel my behaviour has become a lot more open because I do take time to step back. I've realised that I do that more now because it is part of my personality and it is how I want to project myself. It has made me think much more about my interactions with other people I work with – I'm much more considered.*

Understanding of others

This is an appreciation and understanding of the styles and behaviours of others. This attribute relates to a greater understanding of a leader's interpersonal domain. This may include colleagues and clients but is particularly pertinent to the people they lead.

> *I now recognise that a breadth of humanity can be successful in managing information or delivering outcomes. I knew this hypothetically but to be confronted with it by people in the group was another thing altogether. Listening to the others it dawned on me that there is a place for all of those different styles and one is not necessarily better than the other. I guess in the past I made the assumption that everyone functions in pretty similar ways but I realise now that people absolutely don't. It was great to listen to the others, particularly those that function in very different ways to me and hear about how that serves them. I can also identify much more now with how other people around me are operating and on where the strengths of these people lay. To discuss quite deeply about our own experiences of how we operate was so incredibly valuable and I have much greater respect now for other people than perhaps I did previously.*

Flexible and effective interactions with others

This is an ability to adapt to the styles and behaviours of others. This attribute is the operationalising of the previous one. It is when an individual takes a new understanding of their interpersonal domain and uses this to inform new and more effective ways of communicating and relating to others.

> *It's really helped me understand the team and one guy in particular who just seems to fly off all over the place. He's doing a million things and I really struggle to understand what he's asking me sometimes. But recognising his personality now helps me work better with him. I could have got completely frustrated with him and probably stopped dealing with him, whereas now I'm prepared to take time out to understand what it is he needs me to do for him. I'm much better with challenge as I wasn't as good as I could be with others. Sometimes I didn't exhibit the right behaviour towards them. I think I'm much better at that now and so even quite difficult conversations don't feel like things that are going to get pushed back to a different time – they are now things that we can have in a very mature fashion.*

Leadership capacity and proactivity

This is an active and resilient approach to leadership responsibilities. This attribute is the increase in an individual's ability to manage their workload and with increased resilience as they do so. Without actually teaching new management skills, it appears the process of deep self-reflection removes intrinsic blockers that in turn enable an individual to engage more fully and efficiently with their work.

> *My boss has talked about me being their successor and actually now, I can see that as a distinct possibility. I still think there's a number of hurdles that would have to be overcome, but I don't see them now as absolute blockers. Now I see them just as hurdles that can be got over by my own performance. I can't pick out a point at which I said to myself, "Yes, I'm going to do something about my self-confidence," but something's happened throughout the programme where I've gone, "Yeah, I'm going to have a go at that," and without even thinking about it I've volunteered for various things. That's thrown me into some challenges, but they've all been met OK. Another one of the options going forwards is that I get the entire department reporting into me for the whole site rather than it sitting in each of the directorates. If you'd*

offered me that a few months ago I'd have thought, "Oh my god, do I really want 50 or 60 people now expanding to 100 people working for me... no I don't!" But yeah, I'll give it a go now. I wouldn't have done that before I don't think.

Leadership confidence and clarity

This describes confident and focused leadership. This attribute is a more purposeful and systemic approach to the role of leadership itself, when individuals are beginning to look less at the technical management aspects of their role and more assuredly at the point and purpose of their own leadership responsibility.

I'm much clearer now on why I'm doing what I'm doing. I am much, much clear on what I need to do to be successful in the leadership role I'm doing, both in terms of my team and also in terms of support to my own leadership team. I think I'm much clearer about my expectations from staff and probably have heightened that expectation. I'm much more direct in delivering messages now where in the past I may have used jokes and humour if I'd had to be direct. They now know exactly where they are with me and if I don't like something I tell them very directly, I can now deliver those messages with greater clarity. And they're also stepping up to that too, which is great. But they need the clarity and that's my role.

Strategic orientation

This represents a broad and long term focus on strategic leadership goals. It indicates an increased capacity to turn the previous category into strategic action, taking greater leadership confidence and an increased clarity of purpose and translating this into important and tangible long-term goals. The group coaching offers no 'training' in strategic thinking or strategic planning but, as with the other attributes, it is one that emerges clearly and consistently.

I think how I manage my staff now is better... which means I have a lot more time to do the corporate stuff that I avoided a bit, spending more time looking up rather than just organising down. For example, I started to form this new team of which I am a member and said, "Let's really get the strategy right in terms of what we are here to do. Let's get the programme and schedule of activities right so we know what steps we're going to take to deliver that strategy and then put in place the right machinery, behaviours and culture to deliver these activities to drive that strategy." Because my managers are now clearer on where they're going, we've been offered more work and we are clearer on what we can and can't take on. The growth is sustainable and now it's not the erratic growth as in the past, where we grew very, very quickly and then we lost it very quickly. Now we're back up but it's more strategically considered.

The 4Cs: conscious, confident, competent and congruent

The coding and categorising of the data into demonstrable leadership qualities made it quite clear that they all relate to each other in various ways. For example, an increased understanding of others can help an individual interact more effectively with them. An increase in leadership clarity and confidence can in turn improve strategic leadership, etc. On this basis, a four-component, overarching model was developed (Figures 5.2a and 5.2b). For example, a conscious approach to leadership includes both sub-categories of self-understanding and management mindfulness. Competent leadership involves effective interactions with others and leadership capacity and proactivity. Congruent leadership includes self-understanding and self-management and confident leadership includes leadership confidence and clarity but also strategic leadership.

Once again, I feel compelled to restate that I am not saying this 4C model is what constitutes an authentic leader. I am saying that this group coaching approaching to Authentic Leadership Development can and does help individuals to develop these qualities and become more of: a *conscious leader* who is deliberate and intentional; a *competent leader* who is skilled and able; a *confident leader* who is assertive and self-assured; and a *congruent leader* who is clear and consistent.

So, what does this all actually mean for the leader and those they lead? The empirical, statistical and conceptual evidence presented throughout this book hopefully conveys a real sense of the impact this approach to Authentic Leadership Development has for individual leaders. It illustrates how the group coaching approach can help leaders access and modify their working and core self-concepts, which in turn can lead to considerable personal change, development and growth. These positive adaptations motivate the leader to pursue greater congruence in their behaviour and greater self-concordance in their goals, resulting in greater overall self-determination. Again, it should be remembered that the leaders who participate in AL Group Coaching are intelligent, experienced and motivated professionals who have attended the usual

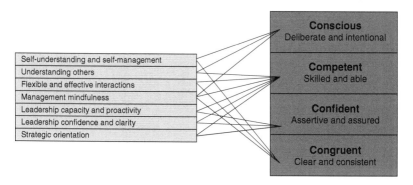

Figure 5.2a Seven leadership attributes linked to the overarching 4C model

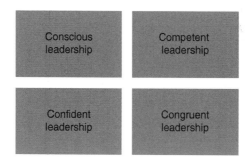

Figure 5.2b The 4C output of Authentic Leadership Group Coaching

suite of L&D programmes, activities and events for much of their career. And so, such leaders are typically at a position in their personal and professional development that makes it clear that the most significant learning about themselves and their leadership will come from within and not from without. A final vignette helps illustrate this point.

> **"A two-way mirror to my values."**
> *David is Director of Informatics for a national government organisation. He is a somewhat rare type of leader in his field in that he leads first and foremost in accordance with his values. This short passage gives an eloquent description of how personal learning can come about in the group not through direct tuition, but through social, vicarious, learning.*

> *"The ALD group work allows you to study how other members feel about their experiences and how you would react to similar experiences. This gives you a two-way mirror. You think, 'This happened to this guy and this is how I would have felt about it, but this is how and why he's feeling about it.' So that is a real learning experience, to understand people's perspectives on events and to compare how you'd deal with them. So as an individual you're reflecting on what you identify with and in the process, you're learning about and clarifying your own values. I class that as real learning – it's not reading from a textbook or having someone tell you how you should feel, think or behave – it's actually you, learning about yourself as a person. You're learning and you're certain you're learning, but you wouldn't describe it as a traditional learning experience."*

This vignette also introduces the topic of personal values which, alongside the more contentious issue of ethics and morals, we move on to discuss in the next chapter.

6 Ethics, morals and values in Authentic Leadership

Ethics and morals

The issue of ethics and morals in Authentic Leadership is a contentious one.[1] The researchers who first developed the main Authentic Leadership construct that currently exists included within it a 'moral perspective' component that they argue should be present in any theory or model of Authentic Leadership.[2] Other researchers pursue this further and propose the moral component is made up of several different facets, such as moral capacity, moral courage and moral resiliency.[3] These same authors speak in quite dramatic terms of how they see the moral responsibility of the Authentic Leader, calling them moral standard-bearers who, "when called upon by the hand of fate, will be the ones who take a stand that changes the course of history for others" (p.248). There are a couple of issues I (and others) have with this. The first is that morals and ethics are normative by nature, in that they are generally adopted standards of correctness in behaviour. The American philosopher and educational reformer, John Dewey, argued that morals are man-made and culturally defined rules that begin outside of the individual and are then gradually inculcated through custom, convention, habit, public opinion and law.[4] This means what is ethical for one individual may well not hold true for another and what is considered moral in one culture or society may not necessarily be transferred to or replicated by another. Consider the images streamed onto the news channels that give us insight into the social, business, political and religious cultures from around the world. It is an ambitious task indeed to distil from all of these existing realities a standard framework of morals and ethics – a framework that could be defined and described and then universally understood, accepted and applied. It is suggested that there are three core aspects to ethical behaviour: justice, fairness and equity.[5] Intuitively, this sounds reasonable, but listening to our televised nightly news debates, it quickly becomes clear that views of what is fair or just are still very subjective.

Next, one has to question the extent to which the idea of moral or ethical leadership is actually an issue for any one particular leader. Of course, there are the visionary leaders mentioned earlier who always come to mind when we think of leadership based around a moral cause or a social change: Nelson Mandela, Mahatma Gandhi, Martin Luther King, for example. But for many leaders, their leadership centres around more earthly concerns, such as the engagement of staff and the delivery of strategic organisational objectives. A higher moral cause or calling simply may not feature in the reality of their everyday leadership experience. They are more concerned with the key issues that support the delivery of these organisational objectives, such as profitability, productivity, customer satisfaction and employee retention.[6] A lot of leaders may do this in line with their own version of the Hippocratic oath of 'do no harm', but beyond that, it may simply not be at the forefront of their mind or their daily leadership. However, that does not mean that they cannot lead in a manner congruent with their deeply held personal *values*. Indeed, whether implicit or explicit, all leadership can be considered to be value laden and value driven, in that an individual's leadership agenda will be inevitably influenced by their own guiding ideas, beliefs and principles.

Values

Values have been described as *abstract ideals* or *trans-situational guiding principles* that direct our choices and behaviours and influence our evaluation of people and events.[7] Put more simply, values consciously and unconsciously mobilise and guide the decisions we make. There are found to be a total of ten core values, presented below, which, unlike morals and ethics, do appear consistent cross-culturally.[8,9] It is important, particularly in a discussion of personal authenticity, to emphasise that these are just value categories and they tell us nothing about what choice of category an individual should make, nor indeed the substantive content of those they do choose (i.e. you may choose ambition or curiosity as a value, but it will be for you to decide what you are ambitious for or curious about). The group coaching approach is very powerful here, in that it doesn't tell you what values you should hold, unlike many so called Authentic Leadership 'training' programmes or texts. If genuine ALD seeks to genuinely develop authenticity, it has to leave the individual leader to be the main author of what it is they genuinely deem as important in terms of their personal values. Let's remind ourselves of what David the Director of Informatics had to say of his ALD group experience in this respect:

> The ALD group work allows you to study how other members feel about their experiences and how you would react to similar experiences. This gives you a two-way mirror. You think, "This happened to this guy and this is how I would have felt about it, but this is how and why he's feeling about it." So that is a real learning experience, to understand people's perspectives on events and to compare how you'd deal with them. So as an individual you're reflecting on what you identify with and in the process, you're learning about and clarifying your own values. I class that as real learning – it's not reading from a textbook or having someone tell you how you should feel, think or behave – it's actually you, learning about yourself as a person."

It's not beyond the realms of possibility that you'll end up discovering that you have a value that is held by or even suggested to you by another, but the point is that you discovered it for yourself and, importantly, you now have an understanding of why it is you hold this particular value. Take honesty, for example – most people might agree that this is a useful and decent value to have and to encourage in the workplace and in teams. But honesty about what? As your manager, I may tell you I'm unconcerned if you help yourself to the contents of the stationery cupboard for your home office. However, I may be quite insistent about transparency in terms of your thoughts, feelings and reactions concerning work-based issues that are important to our team. One is fundamentally different from the other. So, it is important as a leader to understand the genesis of your values so you can genuinely own them and act on them.

In terms of research into values, published findings[10] suggests to us that values generally fall into two main categories: self-enhancement values and self-transcendent values.

Self-enhancement values

* Achievement. Relates to personal success through demonstrating competence, particularly in relation to social standards, and includes ambition/influence/success/skill/intelligence.

- Power. Relates to status, prestige and control over people and resources and includes dimensions such as authority/social power/ social recognition/public image.
- Stimulation. Refers to novelty and challenge in life and includes dimensions such as excitement/variety/daring.
- Self-direction. Refers to independent thought and action in choosing, exploring and creating, including independence/curiosity/goal-autonomy/self-respect/freedom/creativity.
- Hedonism. Centres around personal pleasure and sensuous gratification and includes the dimensions of pleasure/enjoyment.

Self-transcendent values

- Universalism. Refers to understanding, appreciation, tolerance and the welfare of people and nature and includes equality/ peace/wisdom/beauty/nature/broad-mindedness/harmony/social justice.
- Benevolence. Centres around the protection and welfare of the people regularly interacted with, including loyalty/honesty/forgiveness/helpfulness/responsibility/friendship.
- Tradition. Relates to the respect, acceptance and commitment to the customs and ideas that social or cultural tradition provides, including the dimensions of moderation/humbleness/acceptance.
- Conformity. Involves the restraint of impulses likely to cause upset or harm to others or to violate social expectations and norms and includes obedience/politeness/self-discipline.
- Security. Focuses on safety, harmony and stability of relationships, society and self and includes belonging/social order/health/family security/national security.

It is interesting to note that a lot of writers almost instinctively place emphasis on the self-transcendent category of values for Authentic Leaders. Yet some research[11] clearly indicates that self-enhancement values, particularly achievement and self-direction, are both legitimate values in Authentic Leaders. To add to that, the research presented in this book also demonstrates that not only are these perfectly legitimate values (and behaviours), but also they are ones that can be developed. However, in reviewing this list, it becomes apparent that values from both the self-enhancement and self-transcendent categories are reported by leaders who have completed the Authentic Leadership Group Coaching, such as skill, social power and goal autonomy from the self-enhancement category and broad-mindedness, self-discipline and responsibility from the self-transcendence category. But all of this still leaves us with the unanswered question – why do values, ethics and morals even matter for leadership, particularly business leadership?

Ethics, morals and values in business

Ethics has been described as primarily a collective and communal enterprise,[5] the same as organisational life itself – that it only really becomes relevant within a web of relationships, such as a business and the community that business is embedded within and serves. Here, we can see the point and benefits of the three main characteristics said to define ethical behaviour: justice, fairness and equity. Ethics have been described as "how we decide to behave when we decide we belong together" (p.28). They are the standards we use for judging the conduct of one party whose behaviour affects another party and how we protect one person's rights and needs alongside the rights and needs of another. In this context, ethics are not detached from business as business is not detached from life. Business and life have the same bottom line – people (p.29). Business is a human institution and a basic part of the communal fabric of life (p.30). In *Moral Leadership and Business Ethics*, Al Gini argues businesses therefore should ask a fundamental question: "What ought to be done in regard to others?" (p.29).[5] Gini talks of the ethicist, Norman Bowie, who suggests that the existing disconnect between business and ethics comes from the competing world views of economists and ethicists. Economists, Bowie argues, ask, "What can I do to advance my best interests against others?" whereas ethicists ask, "In pursuing my best interests what ought I do in relation to others?" (p.30). One encourages competition and the other cooperation. Therefore, as business is built by and for the human community, the following question should always be considered: what ought to be done in regard to others – those we employ and those we serve? This then leads to the issue of meaning and the purpose that justifies the existence of the business. Naturally, any business should perform well and make a profit, but should that be the ultimate point of its existence? Profit is the life force of a business, as breathing is the life force of a human. But the point of my life, or any life, is not just to breathe. So, should a business's life not be underwritten with some greater meaning and purpose than to simply perform efficiently and make a profit?

Some of the leading business schools seem to think so. Stanford Business School in the USA say their aim of executive education is to "develop innovative, principled and insightful leaders who change the world." Similarly, MIT's Sloan School of Management's aim, is also to "develop principled, innovative leaders who improve the world." Yet most research into leadership effectiveness doesn't measure the impact a leader has had on changing or improving the world. Almost exclusively, the measure of leader effectiveness has become inextricably tied to performance and profit. Meaning, morality or other social issues seem to have become decoupled from the assessment of leader effectiveness, probably because of the difficulty in quantifying them and then correlating them with economic performance. As the authors of *Revisiting the Meaning of Leadership*[12] succinctly put it, "Organisational theory has increasingly concerned itself with phenomena that lend themselves to more straightforward quantification and statistical analysis... ROI makes for a more tractable dependent variable than meaning" (p.74). Thus, economic efficiency has actually emerged as a culturally meaningful and valued end in itself, regardless of the organisation's actual purpose. These scholars argue that when we are concerned about leadership failure, we should not just be concerned about the economic failure of the leader's organisations, but also the moral collapse and associated loss of meaning these failures can engender. They suggest that leadership should provide purpose, meaning and values to an organisation and its members beyond mere technical and economic efficiency. Indeed, it can be argued that a key leadership function is to create such institutionalised meaning and purpose, along with allied values, so as to transform a group of organisational members into a community that finds value and meaning in the pursuit of their objectives.

If higher values, purpose and meaning do not exist within an organisation, then it simply comes down to efficient performance for economic gain, something the German philosopher Weber[5] referred to as *formal rationality*. Formal rationality, he said, was action guided by simple means–ends calculations, as opposed to *substantive rationality*, which is action guided by a belief in the value of the action for its own sake. Consider, for example, the current supply chain product and phenomenon known ominously as *conflict minerals*. Just like the trade in other war economy resources such as *blood diamonds*, this practice is built upon the exploitation and trade in conflict resources during hostilities by commercial entities. Global Witness is an international NGO committed to breaking the link between this natural resource exploitation and the conflict, poverty, corruption and human rights abuses it can spawn. They define such *conflict resources* as those "whose exploitation and trade in a context of conflict contribute to... serious violations of human rights and violations of international humanitarian law" (www.globalwitness.org). Worldwide, there are many *conflict resources* fought over such as fossil fuels and timber, but currently a major target is a mined metal ore from which the element tantalum is extracted and used in the production of capacitors for our laptops, tablets and mobile phones. As one can probably imagine, in developing countries and conflict zones, such mines are often operated by armed groups who illegally tax, extort and coerce civilians and children to work in them. Hegel's idea of formal rationality versus substantive rationality as a guiding principle of leadership even today, maybe particularly today, is still a very cogent one.

A final issue I have with the insistence of many researchers on embedding an ethical or moral component into AL theory is that both of these concepts of leadership already exist independently of Authentic Leadership. They have their own theory, models and even assessment instruments such as the Ethical Leadership Scale.[13,14] Therefore, I remain unconvinced that there is a need for them to be shoehorned into an Authentic Leadership theory, particularly if the research evidence, such as that presented here, does not clearly demonstrate that they are an integral component of Authentic Leadership or Authentic Leadership Development. Other researchers in the field seem to share this view. For example, in the book *Authentic Leadership: Clashes, Convergences and Coalescences*, Eilam-Shamir and Shamir[11] report on research in which they found no particular evidence of a moral perspective in what they believed were the Authentic Leaders they studied. What they did find, however, were very strong indicators that these leaders were motivated by a high need for personal achievements that reflected their deeply held aspirations and passions. They were all leaders who set themselves personally congruent, challenging goals and worked tirelessly to achieve them. However, there was no particular evidence of a higher moral perspective or a socially orientated mission or vision. This led the researchers to ask the following key question directly: "Have we expanded the term authentic leadership to aspects unrelated to authenticity in order to promote a conception of good leadership?" (p.95). Do we consider the leaders in their research to be authentic? I would say yes – they are clearly individuals who enact their self-concepts through the selection and achievement of highly self-concordant behaviours and goals. The absence of an explicitly moral or ethical leadership crusade does not preclude them from acting and being perceived to act as leaders leading in a manner congruent with deeply held personal values, of which achievement and self-direction are two very legitimate examples.

This leaves us with the obvious issue regarding the moral reasoning component of the ALQ and ALI. In their essay 'Authentic leadership and history', Jones and Grint[15] eloquently describe how leadership competencies can develop a contagious and self-referential power. Such competencies are in fact just a series of loose theoretical propositions that can become almost factual over time simply through their progressive layering and refining in the literature. This can result in a construct such as Authentic Leadership, which no longer has its developmental history or component validity scrutinised, but becomes 'black-boxed' and lost to history.[16] These authors argue that each development in the Authentic Leadership literature stacks further refinements of the existing AL competencies one on top of the other, while their origins and validity become ever more hazy and distant. This book is designed in one small way to help arrest the development of this seemingly inevitable trajectory. One contribution to this end is to question the moral reasoning component of the existing AL construct by presenting evidence showing that no such moral or ethical attribute is developed in the process of the AL Group Coaching. Another contribution is to offer several leadership attributes that *are* developed through the process of AL Group Coaching, attributes that include the expected and intuitive, such as increased *self-awareness and self-regulation*, but also those less anticipated, such as an increased *strategic orientation* and increased *leadership capacity and proactivity*. As already mentioned, there is a danger that these could also be considered the basis for an AL competency framework. However, they don't relate to what I propose an Authentic Leader should *be*; rather, they relate to what I know this form of ALD can *develop*. How we measure the impact of this development is the subject of the final chapter.

References

1. Ladkin, D. & Spiller, C. (Eds). (2013). *Authentic Leadership: Clashes, Convergences and Coalescences*. Cheltenham, UK: Edward Elgar Publishing.
2. Walumbwa, F. O., Avolio, B. J., Gardner, W. L., Wernsing, T. S. & Peterson, S. J. (2008). *Authentic leadership: Development and validation of a theory-based measure*. Journal of Management, *34*, 89–126.
3. May, D. R., Chan, A. Y., Hodges, T. D. & Avolio, B. J. (2003*). Developing the moral component of authentic leadership*. Organizational Dynamics, *32*, 247–260.
4. Dewey, J. (1996). *Theory of the Moral Life*. US: Ardent Media.
5. Weber, M. (1964). *The Theory of Social and Economic Organization*. New York: The Free Press.
6. Buckingham, M. & Coffman, C. (2014). *First, Break All the Rules: What the World's Greatest Managers Do Differently*. London: Simon and Schuster.
7. Rokeach, M. (2008). *Understanding Human Values*. New York: Simon and Schuster.

8. Schwartz, S. H. (1994). *Are there universal aspects in the structure and contents of human values?* Journal of Social Issues, *50*, 19–45.
9. Schwartz, S. H. (1992). *Universals in the content and structure of values: Theoretical advances and empirical tests in 20 countries.* Advances in Experimental Social Psychology, *25*, 1–65.
10. Lord, R. G. & Brown, D. J. (2001). *Leadership, values, and subordinate self-concepts.* The Leadership Quarterly, *12*, 133–152.
11. Eilam-Shamir, G. & Shamir, B. (2013). *Life stories, personal ambitions and authenticity: Can leaders be authentic without pursuing the 'higher good'.* In Ladkin, D. & Spiller, C. (Eds). *Authentic Leadership: Clashes, Convergences and Coalescences.* Cheltenham, UK: Edward Elgar Publishing, 93–119.
12. Podolny, J. M., Khurana, R., & Besharov, M. L. (2010). *Revisiting the Meaning of Leadership.* In Nohria, N., & Khurana, R. (Eds.). *Handbook of leadership theory and practice.* Harvard Business Press, 65–105.
13. Brown, M. E. & Treviño, L. K. (2006). *Ethical leadership: A review and future directions.* The Leadership Quarterly, *17*, 595–616.
14. Brown, M. E., Treviño, L. K. & Harrison, D. A. (2005). *Ethical leadership: A social learning perspective for construct development and testing.* Organizational Behavior and Human Decision Processes, *97*, 117–134.
15. Jones, O. S. & Grint, K. (2013). A*uthentic leadership and history.* In Ladkin, D. & Spiller, C. (Eds). *Authentic Leadership: Clashes, Convergences and Coalescences.* Cheltenham, UK: Edward Elgar Publishing, 21–39.
16. Latour, B. (1987). *Science in Action: How to Follow Scientists and Engineers Through Society.* Boston, MA: Harvard University Press.

7   Measuring the impact of Authentic Leadership Development

Hopefully by now you will have a good appreciation of how the group coaching approach to Authentic Leadership Development differs fundamentally from more typical leadership programmes, inasmuch as it is a deeply individual-centric and existentially orientated approach to leadership development. In running these ALD groups, I hear conversations and witness interactions that I rarely experience in regular leadership development programmes. I've observed profound personal change that can be as instant as it is enduring. I know this because as part of this research I kept in touch with some participants for years after their groups had finished and still the changes remain. Such is the power of these peer-based learning groups that some continue to regularly meet years later. So, I know the difference it makes to the individual. And through the analysis presented earlier in this book, I believe I know why this occurs. I also have an understanding of the difference it can make to the leaders' organisations in the form of the seven attributes that have been shown to be developed through this particular approach to ALD. However, I also understand that there will be readers who want to know how to measure such change within their own organisation and so that is the subject of this last chapter, in which we shall explore time-honoured L&D tools such as programme objectives and evaluation levels and their relevance in Authentic Leadership Development.

Objectives

The Holy Grail of organisational L&D has long been to demonstrate its return on investment. The ROI Institute lists several conditions that need to be achieved if a leadership development programme is to be evaluated at the *business impact* and *return on investment* levels.[1] The first step, they say, is to align the programme with the strategic priorities of the organisation and identify the key organisational competencies that are required to achieve these goals. The next step, through a training needs analysis, is to identify the organisational learning needs and specific behaviour changes required to help achieve these organisational aims.

Whilst all of the above may represent sound L&D practice, it is problematic for genuine ALD. By its very nature, Authentic Leadership Development *has* to leave it up to the individual to discover what internal learning and external behaviour change needs to happen to achieve greater congruence within their role as a leader. It is not for anyone else to tell an individual what it is they need to learn to be more authentic. It will always fall to the individual to discover this for themselves.

Traditionally, the next step to ensuring that a programme can be properly evaluated involves the development of the programme objectives, in particular *application* and *impact* objectives. The purpose of these objectives is to state as clearly as possible what trainees are expected to be able to do at the end of their program (p.123).[2] They are usually written from a performance perspective and state how participants should be able to perform in one way or another after the programme is complete and often come with an attached metric such as frequency or quality. The *application* objective defines what the participant is expected to do with what they learn, while the *impact* objective describes what the consequences of this will be. As such, they are highly prescriptive. A traditionally 'well-written' training objective has three elements. It not only states what observable behaviour should be demonstrable by the training delegate after the training course, but also to *what standard* and under *what conditions*. So, not only are they highly prescriptive, but also to a highly granular level. They are historically considered useful for the measurement and evaluation of training programmes, inasmuch as they are closely linked to the competencies identified as missing/needed in the training needs analysis.

Competencies

In essence, competencies are also standard performance indicators. They can be used as a *description of a work task* – what a person has to do in a job – or as a *description of behaviour* – how a person is to do that job (p.5).[3] Like objectives, 'well-written' competencies include *performance indicators* that are in turn composed of *behavioural statements*, so once again they operate at a very high level of specificity. Some organisational competence frameworks even go as far as to include all of the above, in that they detail the *task*, the required *behaviours* and the desired *outputs*. That is a lot of detail, and some may say this falls only slightly short of telling an individual how to put one foot in front of the other!

By now you can probably see the inherent difficulty in applying the concept of competencies and programme objectives to Authentic Leadership Development. If genuine ALD is not to dictate what a leader should learn, then it certainly can't predict how they will apply what they have learnt and what the impact of that will be – frustrating for the L&D or accounting professional perhaps, but not necessarily so for the participant. Experienced, motivated professional leaders at all levels are entrusted in their roles to develop and lead departments, divisions and entire companies. Why should they not be entrusted to assume control over their own personal development? Even at a senior level, leaders are still these days shoehorned into newly developed or even pre-existing leadership competency frameworks. These are issues that bring genuine ALD into potential conflict with the established world of corporate learning and development. Still many organisations I speak to want to know exactly what tools and techniques participants will learn in AL Group Coaching. To me, this betrays either a lack of imagination or a chronic lack of ambition for leadership development – or both. The dumbing down of much typical leadership development seems to have led to a situation where many organisations are happy for their leaders to learn more 'tips and tricks' rather than achieve genuine levels of deep and enduring personal transformation that can lead to paradigm shifts in their perspective and performance i.e. to develop genuinely enhanced levels of confidence and clarity, increased reserves of capacity and resilience, and a new strategic understanding of their leadership role and responsibility. These are not born of tips, tricks, tools or techniques, but fundamental shifts in how individuals see both themselves and their leadership. I therefore don't personally believe the competency and objectives treatment is an appropriate one for Authentic Leadership Development, nor do I believe it is an appropriate one for mature, reflective, intelligent and experienced leaders, such as the type that is appropriate for this form of Authentic Leadership Development.

Evaluation

Another area that potentially sees AL Group Coaching at odds with L&D orthodoxy is the process of programme evaluation. Typically, programme evaluation only tends to capture data at evaluation levels 1 and 2.[4] Level 1 is reaction-level data. It simply gauges participants reactions to the content and format of the programme. This can be interesting for an immediate assessment of a programme's 'face validity' in terms of both content and delivery, but is of questionable value in estimating the impact it will have when the leaders return to work, which, after all, is what it should be all about. Level 2 is learning – this is the new knowledge and insight an individual has gained from participating in a programme. This can be assessed to some degree immediately upon course completion, but again, this is a highly unreliable estimate of what learning will be retained by an individual and, of course, what they will actually do with that learning. That is the purpose of the next level of evaluation. Level 3 evaluation is about application/implementation – this is the extent to which individuals have actually adjusted and changed their behaviours and implemented what they have learnt at level 2. This level of evaluation is critical to understanding what learning from the programme actually makes its way back to the workplace and is implemented by the leader. In this research, level 3 evaluation was conducted by way of one-to-one interviews with each participant three months after the group coaching was complete and resulted in the seven leadership attributes, which are again summarised below, along with the respective evaluation levels they represent. Although not used in this study, it is relevant that we also briefly consider the final two levels of evaluation – levels 4 and 5.

Table 7.1 Evaluation Levels of Leadership Attributes

Leadership attribute		Evaluation level
Raised self-understanding and self-management	2/3	Learning, application and implementation
Greater understanding of others	2	Learning (applied in next attribute)
Flexible and effective interactions with others	3	Application and implementation
Enhanced management mindfulness	2/3	Learning, application and implementation
Increased leadership capacity and proactivity	3	Application and implementation
Heightened leadership confidence and clarity	2/3	Learning, application and implementation
Greater strategic orientation	3	Application and implementation

At level 4 and 5 evaluation, most leadership development programmes run into difficulty. These levels of evaluation attempt to identify the impact of learning and behaviour change on business measures and in turn translate that into a concrete monetary value of return on investment.

Level 4 is impact – this is the consequence of changes implemented at level 3 and usually represents the positive and tangible impact within the leader's own environment, such as increased productivity or quality or decreased time, cost, etc. To evidence a true relationship between the programme and its impact, a direct link *has* to be established connecting the two. This can be notoriously difficult, so the programme and its objectives must be aligned with these specific business measures prior to design and delivery if there is to be any hope of successfully isolating the effects of the programme from other influences impacting the same business measure. In trying to achieve this, the ROI Institute suggests selecting the relevant business impact measures and asking programme participants the following questions: what other factors could have contributed to this performance improvement and, after excluding these, what percentage of the performance improvement can be attributed to the implementation of the programme and, finally, as a percentage, what confidence level is there in that estimate? This can be quite a demanding and complex task and is possibly the reason why a majority of L&D evaluation stops short of this level. In fact, it often stops at level 2, with the typical course evaluation 'happy sheet' given out to delegates before they've even left the premises. As a result, they simply answer typical level 1 and 2 questions, which are variations on: how did you find the programme and what did you learn? It is of course far too early at that stage to say what learning they will apply and how. These are the application and implementation questions of level 3 and can only really be asked a period of time after the programme is complete. According to ROI Institute figures, this is something two-thirds of organisations simply never follow through on, which, in robust evaluation terms, is quite unsatisfactory. Even if there is an excuse for a lack of level 4 evaluation due to time, logistics or cost, there really isn't one for not conducting a level 3 follow-up assessment post-programme to see what behaviour change has actually been achieved, implemented and maintained. This is what was done with the research presented here. The evaluation was conducted three months after the programmes concluded, which was considered imperative to establishing not just what changes were created through AL Group Coaching, but also what changes remained. If you're still doing something differently after three months and it has survived the typical post-programme atrophy, then the chances are very high that it represents a permanent shift in approach and performance.

Level 5 is return on investment – this level of evaluation compares the monetary value of the level 4 impact with the overall cost of the leadership development programme. This is usual accounting practice that can establish the cost/benefit ratio of things like capital equipment, property, etc., but is fraught with complications when trying to assess the same for things like learning and development, where the exact lines of cause and effect within complex organisational systems are so difficult to isolate and correlate. Again, the ROI Institute lays out the steps needed for any project sponsor or organiser interested in attempting this final level of evaluation. These build on the work done at level 4 and require the participants to:

- Decide on a unit of measure (e.g. sale, production, shipment, churn, quality or inventory)
- Determine the value of each unit
- Calculate the change in performance data (after the effects of the programme have been isolated from other influences)
- Determine the annual amount for the change
- Calculate the annual value of the improvement (by multiplying the annual performance change by the unit value)

When so many organisations fail to even attempt a level 3 evaluation, I'm unconvinced that many have the time or inclination to attempt a level 5 ROI assessment and research data seems to support this suspicion. In a recent survey of 96 Fortune 500 CEOs, 92 of them said they were interested in learning the business impact of their leadership development programmes, but only four of them said that was currently happening in their business.[2] ROI Institute research also shows that almost 90 per cent of development programmes are being evaluated at the level 1 reaction level, but only 10 per cent at the level 5 return on investment level.[1] Even level 3 application/implementation evaluation, such as that presented in this research, only accounts for just over a third of evaluations at 34 per cent. So, beyond level 3, where does that leave us with leadership development evaluation generally and Authentic Leadership Development specifically? Well, even the ROI Institute acknowledges that not all programmes should progress to the return on investment level of evaluation, but can still be evaluated by capturing their intangible benefits.

Intangible benefits of Authentic Leadership Development

By definition, most of the benefits of a leader's increased personal and professional authenticity will be felt most keenly by the leader themselves. The benefits witnessed by their followers and organisations will most likely fall into the intangible category. This is not to say that these are of any less importance than the tangible benefits, it is just that they represent benefits even the ROI Institute says cannot, indeed should not, be converted into a monetary value, despite them still providing very important evaluation data. The Institute describes the tangible assets that are required for business operation as, "Readily visible, rigorously quantified, and routinely represented as items on the balance sheet," and intangible assets as, "The key to competitive advantage. But invisible, difficult to quantify, and not tracked through traditional accounting practices" (p.196). One obvious example of an intangible benefit is employee satisfaction, which can be monitored and analysed as a health check of an organisation, but without any further attempt needed to convert the data into a monetary value. Other intangible benefits include such things as:

- Staff and stakeholder engagement
- Positive organisational citizenship behaviour
- Strong organisational reputation
- Job satisfaction
- Team empowerment and motivation
- Positive company culture
- Cooperative team climate

The benefits analysed in this research were mostly of the intangible type, which led to the leadership attributes of self-awareness, self-regulation, clarity, confidence, etc. In this data, there were consistent reports of individuals experiencing a greater confidence in their leadership and clarity about what their leadership responsibilities should involve. Many reported a sudden ability to lift their gaze from up out of the knotty weeds of their day-to-day problems towards the horizon, where they could see and appreciate the longer-term, more complex and systemic issues that they should be focusing on as part of their leadership. Many others reported feeling (re)energised to such a degree that they went for promotions they lacked the confidence (or clarity) to pursue before. Others took on additional responsibilities and projects and yet still felt more resilient and in control than they had previously, even with the additional work. These all describe very striking, albeit intangible, benefits.

In summary, a competency and objective-centric leadership programme is not a leader-centric programme and therefore, in my view, does not constitute genuine Authentic Leadership Development. By definition, that sort of approach prioritises one particular leadership model as best-in-class that will apparently function effectively for a variety of leaders across a variety of leadership situations (p.720).[5] But different leadership roles, across different functions, in different organisations and in different sectors will all require different leaders with different capabilities and different qualities. And after all, what makes great leaders great, at any level, are indeed their differences and not their similarities.

References

1. Phillips, J., Phillips, P. P. & Ray, R. L. (2012). *Measuring Leadership Development: Quantify Your Program's Impact and ROI on Organisational Performance*. New York: McGraw Hill.
2. Buckley, R. & Caple, J. (1995). *The Theory and Practice of Training*. London: Kogan Page.
3. Whiddett, S. & Hollyforde. S. (2003). *Competencies: How to Enhance Individual and Organisational Performance*. London: Chartered Institute of Personnel and Development.
4. Phillips, P. P., Phillips, J. J., Stone, R. D. & Burkett, H. (2007). *The ROI Field Book: Strategies for Implementing ROI in HR and Training*. Oxford: Elsevier.
5. Conger, A. (2010). *Leadership development interventions: Ensuring a return on the investment*. In Nohria, N. & Khurana, R. (Eds). *Handbook of Leadership Theory and Practice*. Boston, MA: Harvard Business School Publishing Corporation, 709–738.

Conclusion

You may have noticed that throughout this book I have not proffered a full definition of Authentic Leadership. I believe to do so would run contrary to the book's central tenets. The best I can offer is that an Authentic Leader is true to their self-concept. They understand who and what they are and they lead in a manner congruent with the values and beliefs that make up that self-concept. However, due to the complexities of organisational life, the Authentic Leader will undoubtedly at times have to compromise on their absolute ideals and make pragmatic judgements and judicious decisions. But as the renowned psychologist Erik Erikson noted: authenticity is not binary, but exists on a scale. You are not either-or – you are more or less.

As is usual, the research presented in this book attempts to convince host organisations of the benefits of leadership development. However, when it comes to Authentic Leadership Development, I personally believe we should, in equal measure, focus on the leaders themselves as well as the organisation. How are they experiencing their role and responsibilities? What makes them more comfortable and confident in their role? Which of their unique qualities and talents can make a difference in their tenure as leader? And of course, how can they bring their self more fully into their role as a leader? The benefit of which is that during stormy conditions, a leader retains sight of their guiding light, what Bill George calls their True North. And the time is propitious, for these are indeed stormy times as we enter ever deeper into what has become known as a VUCA world. Political, social, technological and economic changes are all creating an increasingly multilateral and multivariate world characterised by conditions that are volatile, uncertain, complex and ambiguous – a world where leaders need to actively engage with unpredictability rather than try to control it and start to use intuition alongside logical analysis. As the *disrupters* of Silicon Valley are showing us, in the twenty-first century, it is definitely *not* business as usual but business characterised by these global VUCA conditions.

Volatile conditions that are unexpected and unstable. Conditions impacted by the forces of increased globalisation that augment the speed, scale and volume of change that organisations face and will continue to face. Think geopolitics. *Uncertain* conditions that actually decrease an organisation's awareness, insight or understanding of the issues and events effecting their business and markets – think Uber and Airbnb. *Complex* conditions which are demanding and confusing and have multiple interconnected and potentially confounding elements. Think the North Korean arms race or the apparent influence of Russia in the US election. And *ambiguous* conditions that exist when causal relationships are fundamentally unclear and confusing and we face what Donald Rumsfeld famously called the *unknown unknowns*.

The new century brings with it change that is exponential and laden with multiple meanings, and under such conditions, a leader has to demonstrate together both insight and foresight. They have to plan amidst the confusion, process exorbitant amounts of information and yet make agile decisions. But while being buffeted by the turbulent conditions of a VUCA world, the Authentic Leader remains focused on their leadership purpose and the goals that have value and meaning for them. Performing in a seemingly chaotic world, they are the leaders who are able to clearly see and communicate their leadership vision and, in this respect, are the leaders who will help organisations survive and thrive in the new century.

Index

For Product Safety Concerns and Information please contact our EU representative GPSR@taylorandfrancis.com Taylor & Francis Verlag GmbH, Kaufingerstraße 24, 80331 München, Germany

Printed and bound by CPI Group (UK) Ltd, Croydon, CR0 4YY

11/04/2025

01844008-0002